Idaho à la cARTe

A Gallery of Treasures, Traditions and Tastes
from the Beaux Arts Société

Cover Photograph
Little Redfish Lake,
Sawtooth Mountains
Photograph by Steve Bly, 1994

The jagged peaks of the Sawtooths,
Are pinnacles pointing high
Cleaving the azure heaven,
Wind blown clouds drifting by;
With pine fringed lakes reflecting
Skies of cerulean blue,
Rock castles, forest grandeur,
Wild flowers of every hue.
　　　　　　　—Della Adams Leitner

This cookbook is a collection
of favorite recipes, which are not
necessarily original recipes.

Published by the

BEAUX **ARTS** SOCIÉTÉ
BOISE ART MUSEUM

Copyright©1995 Beaux Arts Société
670 South Julia Davis Drive
Boise, Idaho 83702
1-208-345-8330

Library of Congress Catalog
Number: 95-61734
ISBN: 0-9648326-0-7

Edited and Manufactured by
Favorite Recipes Press®
P.O. Box 305142
Nashville, Tennessee 37230
1-800-358-0560

Manufactured in the United States
of America
First Printing: 1995 15,000 copies

Since 1937, the Boise Art Museum has presented visual arts programs to the citizens of Idaho and its many visitors. Contemporary and historical exhibitions showcasing artists of national and international stature as well as permanent collection highlights are regularly featured. The Beaux Arts Société supports the activities of the Museum with a variety of educational, social, and fund-raising projects. The Société's many dedicated volunteers share a desire to promote the cultural interests of the community and to contribute to the continued success of the Boise Art Museum. Proceeds from the sale of *Idaho à la cARTe* will benefit the Boise Art Museum.

Cookbook Committees

Cookbook Chairman
Kelli A. Catron

Recipe Advisors
Monica Morgan, *Chairman*
Jan Bell
Judy Burroughs
Barbara Erickson
Hazel Haynes
Vicki Helming
Lola Herbots
Suzy Ryder
Bill Selvage
Gloria Shirley
Gerda Weninger
Victoria Wodrich

Recipe Testing
Lola Herbots, *Chairman*
Anne Richey Allen
Jan Bell
Jeanette Bennett
Judy Burroughs
Barbara Emery
Pauline Hinman
Kass Manos
Suzy Ryder
Gloria Shirley
Anne Work

Treasurer
Barbara Erickson

Research and Text
Penny Monger

Editing
Penny Monger, *Chairman*
Barbara Erickson
Colleen Melton
Anne Richey-Allen
Anne Work

Marketing/Sales
Betty Shultz, *Co-Chairman*
Mary Symms, *Co-Chairman*
Lynn Hightower
Amy Rowe
Naomi Tyler
Donna Bari
Susan Cagen
Laurel McClellan
Vicki Helming
Sydney Fidler

Marketing Plan
Mary Symms

Menu Planning
Linda Cadwell, *Chairman*
Judy Burroughs
Penny Monger
Bill Selvage, *Wine Chart*
Betty Shultz

Graphics/Design
Mary Bolen, *Chairman*
Linda Jones
Tonia Ginkle
Penny Monger

Beaux Arts Société President 1994-1995 Linda Cadwell
Beaux Arts Société President 1995-1996 Monica Morgan

Contents

Acknowledgments

Steve Bly, Idaho photographer, specializes in travel and adventure photography and has been featured in over 125 publications, including *Pacific Northwest Magazine* and *Sunset*. His photographs incorporate his love of backpacking, fishing, skiing, and traveling.
Cover, Gallery Four, Gallery Six

Carol Caster, fine art photographer, is a native Idahoan whose published images of light and water reflect the common and unusual beauty of Idaho's mountainscapes, lakes, and rural country scenes.
Gallery Three

Peg Crist has a degree in photography from Brooks Institute, School of Photography in Santa Barbara, California. Her background includes advertising, illustration, and photography, with over ten years of experience coordinating for motion picture, television, and commercial projects as Film Commissioner for the state of Idaho.
Gallery One

Mark List, photographer and native of Idaho, has been published in various regional magazines. He owns and operates his own commercial photography studio and stock photography business in Boise.
Gallery Two, Gallery Seven, Gallery Eight, Wildflower photograph used in each gallery.

Scott Walters, graphic artist, is an Idaho native who received a Bachelor's Degree of Fine Arts from the University of Idaho. Scott lives in Boise where he specializes in originating designs for silk screen.
Advisor

Steve Welsh is a graduate of Brooks Institute, School of Photography in Santa Barbara, California. Welsh Studios in Boise supplies photography to many local companies as well as to international projects.
Gallery Five

We would like to sincerely thank all of the photographers for their generous contributions on behalf of the Boise Art Museum.

Guide to the Galleries

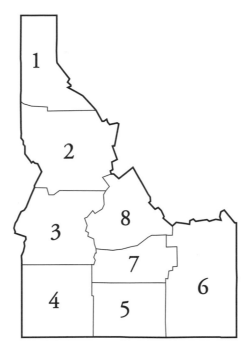

Gallery One North Idaho
Gallery Two North Central Idaho
Gallery Three Southwest Idaho
Gallery Four South Idaho
Gallery Five South Central Idaho
Gallery Six Eastern Idaho
Gallery Seven Central Idaho Rockies
Gallery Eight Northeast Idaho

Gallery One

Appetizers and Beverages

North Idaho

Ice blue lakes, lush emerald pine forests and towering grey
silhouettes—nowhere is the artist's palette more radiant
than North Idaho. Historic mining towns recall times past,
skiers plunge through aspen-lined mountain trails and
the waters beckon to sailors, fishermen and sun-worshippers.

*"There are various types of fir, the white, red and black spruce, scrub oak,
yellow and white pine, mountain mahogany, juniper, and alder…Along the
Clearwater, in Northern Idaho…white pine logs 100" long and red and
white cedar logs 2-5' in diameter are common."*

IDAHO TERRITORY–1881

Cocktail Cruise on Lake Coeur D'Alene

Mine Shaft Beef Satay, page 19

Chicken Bites with Apricot Ginger Sauce, page 14

Gourmet Wrap-arounds, page 26

Creamy Almond and Crab Dip, page 32

Cucumber Dip, page 35, with Vegetable Platter

Round Lake Zucchini and Rice Strudels, page 28

Bruschetta, page 11

Kokanee Smoked Trout Mousse, page 30

White Chocolate Chip Cookies, page 205

Ranchers' Lemon Delights, page 204

Cranberry Margaritas, page 37

Rosé Champagne - Gamay - Sauvignon Blanc

Appetizers
Bruschetta
serves eight

Bruschetta Topping

1¾	pounds fresh plum tomatoes, about 12 to 14 tomatoes
2	tablespoons minced garlic
2	tablespoons minced shallots
1	cup coarsely chopped fresh basil
1	teaspoon balsamic vinegar
⅓	cup olive oil
	Salt and coarsely ground pepper to taste

Bruschetta

8	slices peasant bread
1	clove of garlic, cut into halves
1	tablespoon olive oil

This is especially good during the summer when tomatoes are at their peak.

▲ For the bruschetta topping, chop the tomatoes into ¼-inch pieces. Toss with the minced garlic and shallots in a bowl. Add the basil, vinegar, ⅓ cup olive oil, salt and pepper and mix well. Let stand at room temperature.

▲ For the bruschetta, rub the bread with the cut sides of the garlic and brush with 1 tablespoon olive oil. Grill until toasted.

▲ Arrange the bread on a serving plate and top with the tomato mixture. Serve immediately.

All seem to have agreed with Captain Fremont's recommendation that travelers take plenty of coffee. Of the baggage swept away during an early river crossing, none was looked back upon with such remorse as the drowned coffee ration. "It was a loss which none but a traveler in a strange and inhospitable country can appreciate, and often afterward, when excessive toil and long marching had overcome us with fatigue and weariness, we remembered and mourned over our loss."

FOOD AND FOODWAYS ON THE WESTERN FRONTIER

Marinated Green Beans

serves twelve

Ingredients

2	pounds tender green beans, trimmed
2	tablespoons vegetable oil
2	teaspoons sesame oil
¼	cup rice vinegar
¼	cup soy sauce
1	teaspoon minced garlic
2	tablespoons brown sugar
⅛	teaspoon Tabasco sauce

You may substitute asparagus or other vegetables in season for the green beans in this dish.

▲ Blanch the green beans in boiling water in a saucepan for 2 to 3 minutes. Drain and rinse with cold water. Chill in an airtight container in the refrigerator.

▲ Combine the vegetable oil, sesame oil, vinegar, soy sauce, garlic, brown sugar and Tabasco sauce in a saucepan. Bring to a boil, stirring to mix well.

▲ Add the marinade to the beans. Marinate in the refrigerator for 8 hours or longer, turning or stirring occasionally. Drain to serve or serve with a slotted spoon.

The territorial boundaries of Idaho encompassed a wide variety of geographic features…and her early residents were as diverse as her topography. The Southeast was settled by Mormon missionaries and homesteaders, while the mining and lumber industries attracted rugged individuals to the northern panhandle and central mountain region. The remoteness of the state also attracted a contingent of Civil War veterans, both Yankee and Confederate soldiers, who settled in Idaho mining camps. Northern miners associated themselves with business and culture, while in the south, agricultural communities maintained an alliance with Salt Lake City.

ONE HUNDRED YEARS OF IDAHO ART

Appetizers
Cheese Capers
serves forty-eight

Ingredients

2	cups shredded sharp Cheddar cheese
½	cup mayonnaise
¼	cup sliced green onions with tops
2	tablespoons chopped green olives
1	tablespoon chopped pimento
1	teaspoon chopped capers
6	English muffins, split
⅓	cup grated Parmesan cheese

▲ Preheat the oven to 350 degrees.

▲ Combine the Cheddar cheese, mayonnaise, green onions, olives, pimento and capers in a bowl and mix well. Spread on the cut sides of the muffins. Sprinkle with the Parmesan cheese.

▲ Place the muffins on a baking sheet. Bake for 15 to 18 minutes or until bubbly. Cut into quarters to serve.

In the North Idaho woods, Mary Duffill Donaldson didn't have to depend on a corner grocery market for ingredients for her favorite dish. Beaver tail soup was her rare treat. "Skink, beaver, otter, grouse, geese, rabbit, you name it," she said. "We ate a lot of beaver meat…the tail is the 'pork loin' of the beaver." Mary's favorite cooking oil was made of deer tallow fried out and bear fat from a young black bear. The oil from a brown bear or grizzly bear was too strong.

IDAHO WOMEN IN HISTORY

Chicken Bites with Apricot Ginger Sauce

serves eight

Apricot Ginger Sauce

1	(13-ounce) can apricots
1	(½-inch) piece of ginger, peeled, shredded
1	tablespoon soy sauce
2	teaspoons cornstarch
1	tablespoon cold water
1	green onion, sliced

Chicken

4	chicken breasts, skinned, boned
2	tablespoons butter
1	tablespoon vegetable oil

▲ For the sauce, drain the apricots, reserving a small amount of the syrup. Combine the reserved syrup with the ginger and apricots in a food processor container and process until smooth.

▲ Combine with the soy sauce in a saucepan and mix well. Stir in a mixture of the cornstarch and cold water. Cook until thickened, stirring constantly. Stir in the sliced green onion.

▲ Cut the chicken into bite-size pieces. Rinse and pat dry. Sauté in the butter and oil in a skillet for 5 minutes or until golden brown. Remove to a serving dish. Spoon the sauce over the top.

Women played an important, if unsung, role in producing early western landscapes and western subjects. Their works are lesser known because they did not serve as official expedition artists with government surveys, nor were they among the itinerant artists who crisscrossed the state. Most came to Idaho as wives or family members…the more accomplished women artists who came to the mining camps and early towns had been educated in eastern art schools. Often they were particularly independent individuals, supportive of suffragette causes and prohibition…

ONE HUNDRED YEARS OF IDAHO ART

Chicken Wings with Garlic and Honey

serves eighteen

Ingredients

3	pounds chicken wings
½	cup ketchup
¼	cup water
¼	cup honey
¼	cup red wine vinegar
2	tablespoons brown sugar
2	tablespoons Tabasco sauce
1	tablespoon Dijon mustard
1	tablespoon Worcestershire sauce
1	tablespoon soy sauce
2	cloves of garlic, minced
2	tablespoons onion flakes

▲ Preheat the broiler. Cover a broiler pan with foil and pierce holes in the foil.

▲ Cut each chicken wing into 3 parts, discarding the tips. Rinse chicken and pat dry. Arrange on the prepared pan. Broil just until light brown.

▲ Combine the ketchup, water, honey, vinegar, brown sugar, Tabasco sauce, mustard, Worcestershire sauce, soy sauce, garlic and onion flakes in a saucepan. Simmer for 5 to 10 minutes or until of the desired consistency.

▲ Reduce the oven temperature to 375 degrees. Dip the chicken into the sauce with tongs and arrange on a baking sheet. Bake for 35 to 40 minutes or until cooked through, basting with the remaining sauce. Set oven to broil again and broil wings for several minutes or until crisp.

Beginning in the 1840s, expeditions to the Far West were usually accompanied by artists… The spectacular scenery witnessed by these artist-explorers was recorded in illustrated government reports, and their graphic descriptions of the West were among the first to be published.

ONE HUNDRED YEARS OF IDAHO ART

Ingredients

½	cup shredded Swiss cheese
1	hard-cooked egg, chopped
3	tablespoons fine dry bread crumbs
½	clove of garlic, minced
2	tablespoons butter, softened
1	pound (1- to 1½-inch) mushrooms
¼	cup melted butter

▲ Preheat the broiler.

▲ Combine the cheese, egg, bread crumbs, garlic and softened butter in a bowl and mix well.

▲ Remove the mushroom stems and arrange the caps stem side down on a baking sheet. Brush with the melted butter. Broil for 2 to 3 minutes. Turn the caps.

▲ Fill with the cheese mixture. Broil for 1 to 2 minutes longer.

In North Idaho's Priest Lake area, Molly Moyer and Fern Geisinger annually canned jars and jars of mushrooms. At first, Fern was afraid of mushrooms until someone told her to watch squirrels and eat only the kind the squirrels gathered. Also, she learned to put a penny in the mushroom jar and if the penny turned green, the mushrooms were poisonous and should be buried.

IDAHO WOMEN IN HISTORY

Star Garnet Gougere Wreath

serves eight

Ingredients

¾   cup milk
⅓   cup unsalted butter
½   teaspoon salt
1   cup flour, sifted
3   eggs
7   ounces Gruyère cheese, finely
    chopped
1   egg
½   teaspoon salt

This puffed cheese pastry wreath is a beautiful presentation, but the batter can also be piped into individual baking dishes. Reduce the baking time to eight minutes at 450 degrees and eight minutes at 425 degrees.

▲ Preheat the oven to 425 degrees. Grease a baking sheet.

▲ Bring the milk, butter and ½ teaspoon salt to a boil in a saucepan. Add the flour all at once and mix well. Cook until the mixture pulls from the side of the pan and forms a ball, stirring constantly. Cool slightly.

▲ Place the mixture in a food processor container and add 3 eggs 1 at a time, processing well after each addition. Add 5 ounces of the cheese. Spoon the batter into a 9-inch wreath on the baking sheet or pipe into wreath with a large star point. Brush with a wash of 1 egg beaten with ½ teaspoon salt. Sprinkle with the remaining cheese.

▲ Bake at 425 degrees for 15 minutes. Reduce the oven temperature to 350 degrees. Bake for 10 to 12 minutes. Prick the wreath with a fork. Bake for 5 minutes longer.

Schweitzer Lamb Cocktail Meatballs

serves fifteen

Ingredients

2	pounds ground lamb
⅓	cup soy sauce
½	cup fresh bread crumbs
1	egg, beaten
1	bunch scallions or green onions, chopped
4	cloves of garlic, minced
2	teaspoons minced fresh ginger

▲ Preheat the oven to 375 degrees.

▲ Combine the ground lamb, soy sauce, bread crumbs, egg, scallions, garlic and ginger in a bowl and mix well. Shape into 1-inch balls.

▲ Place on a baking sheet. Bake at 375 degrees for 10 minutes or until golden brown. Serve from a chafing dish warmed by a votive candle.

Cabins were small. In spite of the easy availability of the logs for building, very few of the cabins were built with an eye to the future and the possibility, indeed, the certainty, of the arrival of children. The cabin generally contained room only for a bed, a crude table and box chairs, and a sand box with a tin on top, usually a kerosene can, for a stove. Many…contained crude fireplaces for both heating and cooking.

SALUTE TO PIONEERS OF WASHINGTON AND ADAMS COUNTIES

Appetizers

Mine Shaft Beef Satay

serves eight

Ingredients

½	cup soy sauce
½	cup vegetable oil
3	medium onions, finely chopped
4	cloves of garlic, crushed
2	teaspoons lemon juice
4	teaspoons ground cumin
	Salt and pepper to taste
3	pounds sirloin steak

Serve this on a bed of cilantro garnished with tropical flowers for a summer buffet.

▲ Combine the soy sauce, oil, onions, garlic, lemon juice, cumin, salt and pepper in a large bowl.

▲ Cut the steak into 1-inch cubes. Add to the marinade. Marinate for 8 hours or longer. Drain, reserving the marinade. Thread onto skewers and brush with the reserved marinade.

▲ Grill for 10 minutes or until done to taste, basting frequently with the marinade.

"I do not recall any day that I have felt uncomfortable here. The climate is fine in summer; while it is quite warm in the sun, yet in the shade it is always cool…There is a buoyancy in the step on the people peculiar to those residing in a mountainous region. While the summers are cool and pleasant, the winters are delightful; perhaps not one half of the people in the territory have overcoats…those that do, use them only while riding…"

IDAHO TERRITORY 1881

Chicken and Shrimp Satay with Peanut Sauce

serves eight

Satay

1	cup teriyaki sauce
3½	tablespoons fresh lime juice
4	cloves of garlic, minced
2	tablespoons minced peeled fresh ginger
2	tablespoons brown sugar
1½	pounds boneless skinless chicken breasts
24	medium uncooked shrimp, peeled, deveined

Peanut Sauce

1	cup creamy peanut butter
1	(14-ounce) can chicken broth
¼	cup fresh lime or lemon juice
3	tablespoons brown sugar
2	tablespoons plus 1 teaspoon soy sauce
2	tablespoons chopped peeled fresh ginger
½	teaspoon crushed dried red pepper

The peanut sauce can be prepared up to three days in advance and chilled until needed. Thin it with a small amount of water or chicken broth if necessary and reheat it to serve. It is also good with pasta or pork.

▲ For the satay, combine the teriyaki sauce, lime juice, garlic, ginger and brown sugar in a large bowl, stirring to dissolve the brown sugar. Cut the chicken into ½-inch strips; rinse and pat dry. Add to the marinade with the shrimp, mixing to coat well. Marinate in the refrigerator for 30 minutes to 1 hour. Soak 36 bamboo skewers in water.

▲ Drain the shrimp and chicken. Thread on the skewers. Grill for 3 minutes on each side or until cooked through. Arrange on a platter lined with ornamental kale or lettuce.

▲ For the sauce, combine the peanut butter, chicken broth, lime juice, brown sugar, soy sauce, ginger and red pepper in a saucepan. Cook over medium heat for 5 to 6 minutes, stirring to blend well. Spoon into a bowl and place in the center of the serving platter.

Pend Oreille Pot Stickers

serves eight

Ingredients

11	ounces ground pork
1	cup minced cabbage
2	green onions, minced
1	tablespoon reduced-sodium soy sauce
½	teaspoon grated orange rind
½	teaspoon hot chili oil or chili paste
½	teaspoon salt
40	won ton skins
½	cup peanut oil
1	cup low-fat chicken broth

▲ Combine the pork, cabbage, green onions, soy sauce, orange rind, chili oil and salt in a large bowl and mix well.

▲ Cut the won ton skins into the largest possible circles. Place 1 skin at a time on waxed paper sprinkled with cornstarch. Spoon 1 rounded teaspoonful of the filling in a strip across the center. Moisten the edge and bring opposite sides up to form a semicircle enclosing the filling completely; press edge to seal. Make 3 or 4 pleats toward the center on each side to form a flat-bottomed crescent with a pleated top. Tap lightly on bottom if necessary to make dumpling stand upright. Place on waxed paper sprinkled with cornstarch; cover with towel.

▲ Heat ¼ cup peanut oil in each of 2 heavy 12-inch skillets over low heat. Arrange the dumplings in close rows in the skillets. Increase the heat to medium-high. Cook for 2 minutes or until the bottoms of the dumplings are deep golden brown. Add ½ cup chicken broth to each skillet.

▲ Steam, covered, for 3 minutes or until skins are translucent. Cook, uncovered, until bottoms are very crisp and brown. Loosen with a spatula and remove to a serving dish. Serve immediately with additional hot chili oil and Chinese vinegar or wine vinegar.

Silver Valley Dilled Shrimp

serves ten

Ingredients

1½	cups mayonnaise
⅓	cup lemon juice
½	cup sour cream
¼	cup sugar
1	large red onion, thinly sliced
2	tablespoons dried dill
¼	teaspoon salt
2	pounds medium shrimp, cooked, peeled

It's good that this is so easy to prepare, because no matter how much you make, it won't be enough.

▲ Combine the mayonnaise, lemon juice, sour cream, sugar, onion, dill and salt in a large bowl and mix well. Add the shrimp, stirring to coat well. Chill, covered, for 8 hours, stirring once. Serve with wooden picks.

Marinated Shrimp with Capers and Lemon

serves twenty

Ingredients

4½	pounds shrimp, cooked
1	(2-ounce) jar capers
2	small onions, sliced into rings
2 or 3	lemons, thinly sliced
3 to 4	cups Italian salad dressing
½	cup vinegar
1	tablespoon horseradish
	Celery seeds to taste
6	bay leaves
	Salt to taste

▲ Layer the shrimp, capers, onions and lemon slices in a large bowl. Combine the salad dressing, vinegar, horseradish, celery seeds and bay leaves in a bowl. Pour over the layers. Sprinkle generously with salt.

▲ Marinate in the refrigerator for 24 hours or longer. Discard the bay leaves before serving.

Appetizers

Bonner's Ferry Smoked Turkey in Pumpkin Biscuits

serves twenty-six

Pumpkin Biscuits

2	cups flour
1	tablespoon baking powder
2	tablespoons sugar
1	teaspoon salt
½	cup shortening
2	cups canned pumpkin
2	tablespoons whipping cream

Smoked Turkey Filling

1	pound smoked turkey breast, shredded
4	green onions with tops, chopped
½	cup minced mango chutney
2	tablespoons Dijon mustard
26	spinach leaves or small dark lettuce leaves

This delicious appetizer was served at the Arts for Christmas Preview Night in 1992.

▲ Preheat the oven to 400 degrees.

▲ For the biscuits, combine the flour, baking powder, sugar and salt in a food processor and process until smooth. Add the shortening and pumpkin; process until the mixture forms a very soft dough.

▲ Pat into a ½-inch rectangle on a floured surface. Cut with a 2-inch cutter. Place on a buttered baking sheet and brush with cream. Bake at 400 degrees for 12 to 15 minutes or until golden brown. Cool on a wire rack.

▲ For the filling, combine the turkey, green onions, chutney and mustard in a bowl and mix well. Place 1 spinach leaf in each split biscuit and fill with the turkey mixture. Arrange on a serving platter.

It is not alone in gold and silver that Idaho possesses great wealth: her rich and fertile valleys are not excelled in any State or Territory, an open and inviting field to the farmer and home seeker…

IDAHO TERRITORY 1881

Cheese and Garlic-Stuffed Tomatoes

serves twenty-four

Ingredients

8	ounces cream cheese, softened
1	tablespoon lemon juice
1	scallion, chopped
2	cloves of garlic, minced
1	cup minced fresh herbs
2	pints cherry tomatoes

▲ Combine the cream cheese, lemon juice, scallion, garlic and herbs in a food processor and process until smooth. Spoon into a pastry bag fitted with a star tip.

▲ Remove the tomato stems and cut an X in the opposite ends; squeeze out the seeds. Pipe the filling into the tomatoes. Arrange on a serving platter and chill until serving time.

Cedar Street Tortilla Roll-Ups

serves fifty

Ingredients

12	ounces fat-free cream cheese
1	(7-ounce) can chopped green chiles
1	(4-ounce) can chopped olives
16	ounces sliced turkey ham, chopped
6 to 8	green onions, sliced
1	(12-count) package thin flour tortillas

▲ Combine the cream cheese, green chiles, olives, ham and green onions in a bowl and mix well. Spread over the tortillas and roll to enclose the filling.

▲ Chill until serving time. Slice each roll into 2-inch pieces and arrange on a serving plate.

Priest Lake Vegetable Wraps

serves ten

Ingredients

1	cup broccoli florets
1	cup cauliflowerets
1	cup thinly sliced onion
2	teaspoons vegetable oil
2 to 3	tablespoons barbecue sauce
½	cup finely grated carrot
½	cup finely grated red cabbage
½	cup finely grated yellow squash
10	(6-inch) flour tortillas
3	tablespoons light mayonnaise
½	cup thinly sliced dill pickles
1	avocado, thinly sliced
½	cup alfalfa sprouts
	Spike seasoning or salt and pepper to taste

This is a good party dish, but it is also a great finger food to take along on a hike, a fishing trip or a picnic.

▲ Steam the broccoli and cauliflower in a saucepan for 5 minutes or until tender. Drain and rinse in cold water. Sauté the onion in the oil in a skillet for several minutes. Add the barbecue sauce. Cook until the onion is tender. Combine the carrot, cabbage and squash in a bowl and mix well.

▲ Heat the tortillas 1 at a time in a skillet over medium heat for 1 minute on each side. Remove to work surface. Spread with mayonnaise. Arrange the broccoli mixture and carrot mixture in rows down the center of each tortilla. Top with the sautéed onions, pickles, avocado, sprouts and seasonings. Roll to enclose the filling and wrap individually in plastic wrap. Store for 2 to 3 days in the refrigerator.

At first, settlers fenced only for gardens and grain, cutting hay anywhere as the grass was so plentiful and in many places as tall as a man on horseback. This valley was a beautiful sight in those days, looking like a beautiful painting.

SALUTE TO PIONEERS OF WASHINGTON AND ADAMS COUNTIES

Turkey Wrap-arounds

3	tablespoons mayonnaise
1	tablespoon ketchup
2	flour tortillas
4	thin turkey slices
1/3	cup shredded Monterey Jack cheese
1/4	avocado, chopped
1	cup shredded lettuce
	Salt and pepper to taste

Beef Wrap-arounds

3	tablespoons mayonnaise
1	tablespoon ketchup
2	flour tortillas
4	thin slices rare roast beef
2	tablespoons finely chopped green onions
2	tablespoons finely chopped peeled, seeded cucumber
1/3	cup shredded Swiss cheese
1/2	cup alfalfa sprouts

To make wrap-arounds, work with one very fresh tortilla at a time, leaving the remaining tortillas covered to prevent drying out.

▲ For the turkey wrap-arounds, mix the mayonnaise and ketchup in a bowl. Spread over the tortillas. Layer the turkey, cheese, avocado and lettuce on the tortillas, sprinkling the turkey with salt and pepper. Roll tightly and wrap in plastic wrap. Chill for 1 to 4 hours. Cut into 4 portions to serve.

▲ For the beef wrap-arounds, mix the mayonnaise and ketchup in a bowl. Spread over the tortillas. Layer the roast beef, green onions, cucumber, cheese and alfalfa sprouts on the tortillas. Roll tightly and wrap in plastic wrap. Chill for 1 to 4 hours. Cut each roll into 4 portions to serve.

▲ You can also make smoked salmon wrap-arounds with 3 ounces cream cheese, 4 ounces sliced smoked salmon and 2 tablespoons each of chopped green onions, tomato and cucumber. For ham wrap-arounds use 4 thin slices of ham, 1 tablespoon of mayonnaise, 1 tablespoon of Dijon mustard, 1/2 cup shredded Cheddar or Swiss cheese, 2 tablespoons chopped green chiles and 1/4 chopped avocado.

Cataldo Mission Vegetarian Pizza Delight

serves fifteen

Ingredients

1	(8-ounce) can crescent rolls
8	ounces cream cheese, softened
¼	cup mayonnaise
¼	teaspoon dillweed
½	envelope ranch salad dressing mix
½	cup chopped green onions
1	cup chopped seeded tomatoes
½	cup chopped peeled cucumber
½	cup chopped zucchini
½	cup sliced olives

Vary the toppings of this pizza to suit your fancy and the fresh vegetables in season.

▲ Unroll the crescent roll dough and press into a 9x13-inch baking pan, pressing the edges and perforations to seal. Bake using the package directions. Cool to room temperature.

▲ Combine the cream cheese, mayonnaise, dillweed and salad dressing mix in a bowl and mix well. Spread over the cooled crust. Sprinkle with the chopped vegetables and olives, pressing lightly into the cream cheese mixture. Chill until serving time. Cut into squares to serve.

Jesuit missionaries were responsible for establishing the first church settlements among the Flathead and Coeur D'Alene Indians of northern Idaho. The DeSmet expedition entered this area in 1840 accompanied by French artist and architect Father Nicholas Point. They were the founders of the Cataldo Mission, Idaho's oldest standing building...

ONE HUNDRED YEARS OF IDAHO ART

Round Lake Zucchini and Rice Strudels

serves twelve

Ingredients

1	small onion, chopped
1	clove of garlic, minced
2	tablespoons butter
4	ounces zucchini, grated
4	ounces brown rice, cooked
1	ounce sliced almonds, toasted
½	egg, beaten
1 to 2	tablespoons crème fraîche or sour cream
1	ounce Parmesan cheese, grated
½	teaspoon thyme
	Salt and pepper to taste
4	sheets phyllo dough

▲ Sauté the onion and garlic in 1 tablespoon butter in a skillet for 5 minutes. Add the zucchini and sauté for 5 minutes longer. Combine with the rice, almonds, egg, crème fraîche, cheese, thyme, salt and pepper in a bowl and mix well. Chill for 30 minutes.

▲ Melt the remaining butter in a saucepan. Place 1 phyllo sheet on a work surface and brush with the melted butter. Top with a second sheet. Spread half the vegetable mixture over the sheets and roll to enclose the filling; seal the edge with the butter. Repeat with the remaining ingredients. Place on a baking sheet.

▲ Preheat the oven to 400 degrees. Bake the strudels for 25 minutes. Slice to serve.

Candles were used when they could be obtained; otherwise, tin cans filled with animal fat and rags for wicks were used. Floors were of packed dirt, and doors were slabbed logs, very heavy and not very tight, so that winter air freely filtered through into the cabin. The walls were 'chinked' with mud, and sometimes kindling wood was forced between the logs.

FOOTPRINTS ON MOUNTAIN TRAILS

Black Bean Salsa with Cilantro and Lime
serves thirty

Ingredients

1	(28-ounce) can black beans, drained, rinsed
1	cup frozen corn
1	(14-ounce) can tomatoes
2	cloves of garlic, minced
1	jalapeño pepper, minced
1	small Spanish onion, chopped
2	medium tomatoes, peeled, seeded, chopped
1	tomatillo, chopped
1	bunch cilantro, chopped
	Juice of ½ lime
1½	tablespoons cumin
¼	teaspoon cinnamon
	Salt, red pepper, cayenne pepper and black pepper to taste
1	tablespoon olive oil
1	tablespoon vinegar

This is great with chips or on omelets.

▲ Combine the beans, corn and canned tomatoes in a large bowl. Stir in the garlic, jalapeño pepper, onion, fresh tomatoes, tomatillo and cilantro.

▲ Add the lime juice, cumin, cinnamon, salt, red pepper, cayenne pepper, black pepper, olive oil and vinegar and mix gently. Chill for 8 hours or longer.

Even though they produced much of what they consumed and made many of the articles their living required – all their clothes except overalls were made from yard goods – a subsistence economy still required a certain amount of currency…The sale of cream was an important source of income, no matter how small.

IDAHO FOLKLIFE: HOMESTEADS TO HEADSTONES

Post Falls Smoked Salmon Spread

serves eight

Ingredients

8	ounces cream cheese
¼	cup whipping cream
1	scallion, thinly sliced
1	teaspoon fresh lemon juice
	Tabasco sauce to taste
4	ounces smoked salmon, shredded
2	tablespoons red salmon caviar

▲ Combine the cream cheese and cream in a bowl and mix gently until smooth. Stir in the scallion, lemon juice and Tabasco sauce. Fold in the salmon and caviar. Serve on thinly sliced French bread.

Kokanee Smoked Trout Mousse

serves fifteen

Ingredients

1	envelope unflavored gelatin
2	tablespoons lemon juice
½	cup boiling water
1	small slice onion
10	ounces smoked trout
½	cup mayonnaise
1	tablespoon Dijon mustard
	Tabasco sauce to taste
1	cup whipping cream

▲ Sprinkle the gelatin over the lemon juice in a food processor. Let stand for several minutes. Add the boiling water and onion and process for 40 seconds. Add the trout, mayonnaise, mustard and Tabasco sauce and process until smooth. Add the cream ⅓ at a time, processing after each addition until smooth.

▲ Spoon into a 4-cup mold. Chill until set. Unmold onto a serving plate. Serve with rye or pumpernickel rounds or crackers.

Appetizers

Thyme and Garlic Spread

serves sixteen

Ingredients

16   ounces cream cheese, softened
¼   cup white wine
2 to 4   cloves of garlic, minced
1   teaspoon lemon juice
3 to 4   tablespoons thyme
1½   teaspoons seasoned salt
     Pepper to taste

▲ Combine the cream cheese, wine, garlic, lemon juice, thyme, seasoned salt and pepper in a bowl and mix until smooth. Chill in the refrigerator.

▲ Serve with sourdough bread rounds or crisp crackers.

Cream Cheese Spread with Sun-Dried Tomatoes and Basil

serves sixteen

Ingredients

8   oil-pack sun-dried tomatoes, drained
8   fresh basil leaves
16   ounces low-fat cream cheese, softened

▲ Rinse the sun-dried tomatoes and combine with the basil in a food processor; process until puréed. Add the cream cheese and process until smooth. Chill for several hours.

▲ Let stand at room temperature for 1 hour before serving. Serve with crackers or bread slices.

Creamy Almond and Crab Dip

serves eight

Ingredients

8	ounces cream cheese, softened
1	tablespoon milk
1	cup fresh crab meat
2	green onions, finely chopped
1	tablespoon minced fresh parsley
1	teaspoon Worcestershire sauce
1	teaspoon fresh lemon juice
	Tabasco sauce to taste
¼	teaspoon salt
¼	cup sliced almonds, toasted

▲ Preheat the oven to 375 degrees.

▲ Combine the cream cheese, milk, crab meat, green onions, parsley, Worcestershire sauce, lemon juice, Tabasco sauce and salt in a mixer bowl and beat with a hand mixer until well mixed. Spoon into a small soufflé dish.

▲ Bake at 375 degrees for 20 to 25 minutes or until bubbly. Sprinkle with the toasted almonds. Serve with plain Melba rounds.

▲ You may prepare this dip in advance, cover with plastic wrap and chill until baking time.

At first, before roads, pack trains carried freight, as well as passengers, to their destinations. Many ladies, and perhaps even men, who had in all probability never been on a saddle horse before, were initiated into that style of transportation with varying degrees of anticipation and discomfort.

SALUTE TO PIONEERS OF WASHINGTON AND ADAMS COUNTIES

Hot Artichoke Dip with Parmesan Cheese

serves twelve

Ingredients

1	(14-ounce) can artichoke hearts, drained, chopped
1	(4-ounce) can green chiles, rinsed, seeded, chopped
1	cup grated Parmesan cheese
1	cup mayonnaise or mayonnaise-type salad dressing

▲ Preheat the oven to 350 degrees.

▲ Combine the artichoke hearts, green chiles, cheese and mayonnaise in a bowl and mix well. Spoon into an 8-inch round baking dish.

▲ Bake at 350 degrees for 20 minutes or until heated through. Serve warm with tortilla chips and bread sticks.

Emerald Creek Bleu Cheese Dip

serves six

Ingredients

⅓	cup sour cream
⅓	cup mayonnaise
1	tablespoon fresh lemon juice
1	clove of garlic, crushed
½	cup chopped fresh spinach
½	cup Danish bleu cheese, crumbled
¼	teaspoon tarragon
1	teaspoon dried dill

▲ Combine the sour cream, mayonnaise, lemon juice, garlic, spinach, bleu cheese, tarragon and dill in a bowl and beat with a hand mixer until well mixed. Spoon into a small serving dish.

▲ Chill for 2 to 12 hours. Serve with small crackers or chips.

Appetizers

Kootenai Cheese Dip

serves twenty

Ingredients

2	pounds Velveeta cheese, chopped
1½	(8-ounce) jars cream-style horseradish
1	cup plus 2 tablespoons mayonnaise
10	drops of Tabasco sauce
5	ounces beer

▲ Combine the cheese, horseradish, mayonnaise and Tabasco sauce in a double boiler. Heat over hot water until the cheese melts, stirring to mix well. Stir in the beer.

▲ Serve at room temperature with chips. You may store this in the refrigerator for several days.

Coeur D'Alene Caviar

serves sixteen

Ingredients

2	large tomatoes, chopped
2	(4-ounce) cans chopped black olives
1	(8-ounce) can chopped green chiles
4 to 6	green onions, chopped
1 or 2	jalapeño peppers, chopped (optional)
1½	tablespoons vinegar
3	tablespoons olive oil
1	teaspoon garlic powder
½	teaspoon salt
	Tabasco sauce to taste

▲ Combine the tomatoes, olives, green chiles, green onions, jalapeño peppers, vinegar, olive oil, garlic powder and salt in a bowl and mix well.

▲ Season to taste with Tabasco sauce and serve with tortilla chips.

Cucumber Dip

serves ten

Ingredients

8	ounces cream cheese, softened
1	tablespoon mayonnaise or mayonnaise-type salad dressing
1	teaspoon MSG (optional)
⅛	teaspoon garlic salt
¾	teaspoon salt
	Pepper to taste
¾ to 1	cucumber, chopped
3 or 4	scallion bulbs, chopped

▲ Combine the cream cheese, mayonnaise, MSG, garlic salt, salt and pepper in a mixer bowl and beat until smooth. Stir in the cucumber and scallions.

▲ Spoon into a serving bowl. Chill, covered, for 30 minutes or longer. Serve with fresh vegetables, chips or crackers.

Dilled Crackers

serves twelve

Ingredients

1	(11-ounce) package oyster crackers
1	envelope ranch salad dressing mix
½	teaspoon dill
½	teaspoon lemon pepper
½	teaspoon garlic powder
⅔	cup peanut oil

Great to have on hand as a snack when lots of people are around.

▲ Preheat the oven to 225 degrees. Spread the oyster crackers in a roasting pan.

▲ Combine the salad dressing mix, dill, lemon pepper, garlic powder and peanut oil in a bowl and mix well. Pour over the crackers, stirring to mix well.

▲ Bake at 225 degrees for 35 to 40 minutes or until golden brown, stirring occasionally. Cool completely and store in an airtight container.

Glazed Almonds

serves thirty-two

Ingredients

4	egg whites
½	cup Champagne
2	cups sugar
2	teaspoons salt
1	tablespoon cinnamon
8	cups whole almonds

▲ Preheat the oven to 250 degrees. Spray two 10x15-inch baking pans with nonstick cooking spray.

▲ Whisk the egg whites lightly in a large bowl. Add the Champagne, sugar and salt; whisk until smooth. Add the cinnamon and almonds and mix until well coated. Spread in prepared baking pans.

▲ Bake at 250 degrees for 1 to 1¼ hours or until the nuts appear dry, stirring occasionally. Remove to waxed paper-lined racks and separate almonds with 2 forks. Let stand until cool. Store in airtight container.

▲ For gingered pecans, substitute 1 teaspoon ginger for 1 teaspoon of the cinnamon and pecan halves for the almonds.

▲ For five-spice walnuts, use 1 teaspoon cinnamon, 1 teaspoon nutmeg, ½ teaspoon ginger, ¼ teaspoon cloves and ¼ teaspoon allspice with 8 cups walnut halves.

Silver Mountain Margaritas

serves twelve

Ingredients

1	(6-ounce) can frozen limeade concentrate, thawed
3	(6-ounce) cans water
¾	(6-ounce) can Triple Sec
1	(6-ounce) can tequila

This is delicious to keep on hand in the freezer.

▲ Combine the limeade concentrate, water, Triple Sec and tequila in a pitcher and mix well. Freeze until slushy. Serve over ice in glasses.

Cranberry Margaritas

serves six

Ingredients

1¼	cups cranberry juice cocktail
½	cup sugar
1½	cups fresh or frozen cranberries
¾	cup lime juice
¾	cup tequila
½	cup orange liqueur
3	cups coarsely crushed ice

Festive for the holidays.

▲ Pour ¼ cup of the cranberry juice into a shallow bowl. Pour 3 tablespoons of the sugar onto a flat plate. Dip the rims of 6 wide-mouthed glasses into the juice and then into the sugar to coat the rims.

▲ Reserve 12 cranberries. Combine the remaining cranberries with the remaining cranberry juice, remaining sugar, lime juice, tequila, orange liqueur and ice in a bowl and mix well. Process in 2 batches in a blender until smooth. Pour into prepared glasses and garnish with the reserved cranberries.

Fourth of July Pass Caffé Latté Punch

serves sixteen

Ingredients

½   cup sugar

1   quart strong coffee

1   pint vanilla ice cream, softened

3   tablespoons coffee brandy

2   cups whipped topping or whipped cream

Nutmeg to taste

▲ Dissolve the sugar in the coffee in a pitcher. Chill for 24 hours.

▲ Combine with the ice cream and brandy in a punch bowl; let stand for 15 minutes. Fold in the whipped topping. Sprinkle the servings with nutmeg.

Lookout Pass Fruit Punch

serves fifty

Ingredients

3   (12-ounce) cans frozen apple juice concentrate

2   (12-ounce) cans frozen orange juice concentrate

1   (12-ounce) can frozen pineapple juice concentrate

4   (12-ounce) cans water

1   (2-liter) bottle ginger ale or 7-Up

▲ Combine the apple juice concentrate, orange juice concentrate, pineapple juice concentrate and water in a large container and mix well. Chill in the refrigerator.

▲ Combine with the ginger ale in a punch bowl and mix gently.

Beverages

Spiced Cranberry Punch

serves sixteen

Ingredients

1	cup sugar
4	cups water
12	whole cloves
4	(3-inch) cinnamon sticks
2	tablespoons minced gingerroot
8	cups cranberry-apple juice cocktail
2	cups orange juice
1	cup fresh lemon juice
1½	cups spiced or dark rum (optional)

This can also be chilled for up to two days and served cold in a punch bowl with ice cubes made of additional cranberry juice, orange slices and cranberries.

▲ Combine the sugar, water, cloves, cinnamon sticks and ginger in a large saucepan. Bring to a boil and simmer for 10 minutes. Let stand, covered, for 1 hour.

▲ Strain the mixture into a large bowl. Stir in the cranberry-apple juice, orange juice and lemon juice. Reheat to serve hot and stir in the rum.

Champagne Punch

serves twenty-four

Ingredients

1½	quarts sauterne or Rhine wine
⅔	cup brandy
2	fifths Champagne
⅓	cup sugar

▲ Chill the wine, brandy and Champagne in the refrigerator. Combine with the sugar in a punch bowl and mix gently to dissolve the sugar.

Gallery Two

Salads

North Central Idaho

2.3 million acres of designated wilderness, biggest in the
lower 48; Hell's Canyon, sculpted deeper than the Grand
Canyon; and the Palouse, some of the richest farmland
in the West; all inspire the creativity of the spirit and
the contemplation of the poet.

*"Tourists will find much to interest them in Idaho—Placid valleys basking in
sunshine, with gigantic snow-clad mountains towering in the background; bold,
dashing rivers,…streams with myriads of trout and other fish disporting in their
transparent depth, or waterfowl covering their placid surface…all are here."*

IDAHO TERRITORY–1881

Hells Canyon River Trip

Marinated Shrimp with Capers and Lemon, page 22
Pinot Noir Blanc

Baked Vegetables Provençal, page 89

Oregon Trail Barbecued Lamb, page 129

Mountain Home Marinated Steak, page 125
Merlot

Hull's Gulch Potatoes Boulangerie, page 100

Float Trip Disappearing Chocolate Bars, page 203

Whitewater Spicy Bean Cake, page 197

Lewis and Clark Arugula and Orange Salad

serves four

Salad

1	bulb fennel, cut lengthwise into quarters
2	medium oranges
2	bunches arugula, trimmed
1	red onion, sliced into thin rings
3	radishes, thinly sliced
2	ounces Parmesan cheese, grated

Lemon Dressing

3	tablespoons olive oil
2	tablespoons fresh lemon juice
1	clove of garlic, crushed
¼	teaspoon salt
	Freshly ground pepper to taste

There are three secrets to the success of this salad: use only fresh lemon juice in the dressing, slice the onion very thin and use imported Parmesan cheese.

▲ For the salad, soak the fennel in ice water for 20 minutes. Drain and pat dry. Cut into thin slices. Cut the oranges into halves lengthwise and slice. Combine the fennel, oranges, arugula, onion and radishes in a salad bowl.

▲ For the dressing, whisk the olive oil, lemon juice, garlic, salt and pepper in a bowl.

▲ Add the dressing to the salad and toss to mix well. Top with the cheese.

We came from no country, as have the whites.
We were always here.
Nature placed us in this land of ours.

Yellow Wolf, Nez Perce Leader
WAY OUT IN IDAHO

Elk Creek Asparagus and Prosciutto Salad

serves six

Salad

1	pound fresh asparagus
4	ounces Gouda cheese, cut into ½-inch cubes
1	(4-ounce) jar whole mushrooms, drained
½	small red onion, thinly sliced
2	ounces prosciutto, cut into strips

Dijon Vinaigrette

2	tablespoons olive oil
1	tablespoon red wine vinegar
1	tablespoon fresh lemon juice
1	teaspoon Dijon mustard
1	clove of garlic, minced
1	teaspoon chopped fresh rosemary

▲ For the salad, snap off the tough ends of the asparagus and cut the stalks into 2-inch pieces. Steam the asparagus for 4 to 8 minutes or until tender-crisp. Drain, rinse in cold water and drain again. Chill in the refrigerator. Combine with the cheese, mushrooms, onion and prosciutto in a medium bowl.

▲ For the vinaigrette, whisk the olive oil, vinegar, lemon juice, mustard, garlic and rosemary in a bowl.

▲ Add the vinaigrette to the salad and toss to mix well. Serve immediately or chill until serving time.

"Will had lots of nice lettuce while I was in town last spring…but the birds eat it up before I could have any. We had some nice beans this summer, lots of sweet corn, a few little musk melons and a watermelon or two that didn't amount to anything…there was some spinach last spring too, but I wasn't here to use it so it went to seed…the birds eat the onions that came from the seed and the beet seed didn't come up at all…the birds, squirrels, gophers, rabbits, rats and mice bothered the garden, and the cow got in once and eat the corn, too."

SALMON RIVER SAGA

Bitterroot Herbed Bean Salad

serves six

Herb Dressing

¼	cup lemon juice
¼	cup white wine vinegar
¼	cup olive oil or vegetable oil
1	tablespoon Dijon mustard
1	tablespoon honey mustard
1	small clove of garlic, minced
1	tablespoon chopped fresh basil
1½	teaspoons chopped fresh thyme
½	teaspoon salt
⅛	teaspoon pepper

Salad

3	cups cooked small white beans
1	cup chopped peeled cucumber, seeded
1	cup chopped red bell pepper
2	tablespoons chopped celery
2	tablespoons chopped green onions
2	tablespoons chopped parsley
4 to 8	ounces whole tender green beans, trimmed
6	cherry tomatoes, cut into halves

Compliments of the Idaho Bean Commission.

▲ For the dressing, combine the lemon juice, vinegar, mustards, garlic, basil, thyme, salt and pepper in a bowl and whisk until smooth. Whisk in the olive oil gradually.

▲ For the salad, combine the white beans, cucumber, bell pepper, celery, green onions and parsley in a bowl. Add ½ cup of the dressing and toss to coat well. Let stand at room temperature for 1 hour.

▲ Steam the green beans for 2 minutes or until tender-crisp; drain. Add 2 tablespoons of the dressing to the warm beans.

▲ Arrange the white bean mixture, the green beans and the tomatoes on lettuce-lined salad plates. Serve with the remaining dressing.

Salads

Lolo Pass Coleslaw

serves eight

Dressing

¼	cup chunky peanut butter
1	tablespoon fresh lime juice
1	tablespoon grated gingerroot
2	teaspoons grated garlic
2	teaspoons sugar
1	teaspoon soy sauce
¼	cup water

Salad

2	pounds cabbage, thinly sliced
1	green bell pepper, thinly sliced
1	red bell pepper, thinly sliced
1	medium sweet onion, thinly sliced
1	jalapeño pepper, seeded, minced
½	teaspoon salt
½	cup coarsely chopped dry-roasted peanuts

▲ For the dressing, combine the peanut butter, lime juice, gingerroot, garlic. sugar and soy sauce in a bowl and mix well. Whisk in the water gradually. Let stand at room temperature.

▲ For the salad, combine the cabbage, bell peppers, onion, jalapeño pepper and salt in a bowl and mix well. Chill in the refrigerator. Add the dressing and toss to coat well. Let stand for 2 hours. Add the peanuts and toss gently.

A pony is not an indispensable requisite to a trip of this kind, yet it is advisable for a party to have one along; they can be had cheap at the Missouri River, and will save many a step for the weary immigrant in the way of herding and collecting his stock; and for the purpose of enjoying the buffalo chase or the more daring encounter of the grizzly, the pony is quite indispensable.

BOUND FOR IDAHO

Red Cabbage Salad with Bacon and Goat Cheese

serves six

Salad

1	pound sliced bacon
1	(1-pound) head red cabbage, shredded
5½	ounces Montrachet or other goat cheese, crumbled

Cabbage Dressing

¼	cup reserved bacon drippings
½	cup vegetable oil
¼	cup red wine vinegar
2	cloves of garlic, minced
¼	teaspoon pepper

The red of the cabbage, the crunch of the bacon and the tang of the goat cheese combine for an exceptional salad. Both the salad and the dressing may be prepared in advance and chilled overnight. Bring the salad to room temperature and reheat the dressing to serve.

▲ For the salad, fry the bacon in a skillet until crisp. Drain and crumble the bacon, reserving ¼ cup of the drippings for the dressing. Combine the bacon with the cabbage and goat cheese in a bowl and mix well.

▲ For the dressing, combine the reserved bacon drippings with the vegetable oil, vinegar, garlic and pepper in a saucepan. Heat until heated through.

▲ Pour the dressing over the salad and toss to coat well.

Minted Cucumber Salad

serves eight

Ingredients

4	cucumbers
2	teaspoons salt
1	small green bell pepper, chopped
3	green onions, chopped
¼	cup chopped fresh mint
1	cup plain yogurt
¼	cup lemon juice
2	tablespoons olive oil
2	cloves of garlic, minced

▲ Peel, seed and chop the cucumbers. Sprinkle with salt in a bowl and let stand for 15 minutes. Rinse with cold water and pat dry. Mix with the green pepper and green onions in a bowl.

▲ Combine the mint, yogurt, lemon juice, olive oil and garlic in a bowl and mix well. Add to the salad and toss lightly. Chill, covered, for 30 minutes or longer.

▲ Serve in a salad bowl lined with Bibb lettuce; sprinkle with additional fresh mint.

Fresh Mushroom Salad

serves six

Ingredients

1½	pounds button mushrooms
¼	cup lemon juice
10	tablespoons olive oil
6	tablespoons minced green onions
2	tablespoons chopped chives
¼	cup chopped parsley
	Salt and pepper to taste
6	slices bacon, crisp-fried, crumbled

▲ Slice the mushrooms, discarding the stems. Combine with the lemon juice and olive oil in a bowl. Add the green onions, chives, parsley, salt and pepper; mix lightly. Chill, covered, for 1 hour or longer.

▲ Drain the salad and add the bacon; toss lightly to serve.

Couscous Provençal

serves six

Salad

2	cups water
1	cup uncooked couscous
¼	teaspoon salt
2	large tomatoes, seeded, cut into ½-inch pieces
2	medium green onions, minced
¼	cup chopped celery
8	imported black olives, coarsely chopped
¼	cup minced fresh parsley
¼	cup minced fresh mint

Couscous Dressing

5	tablespoons fresh lemon juice
2	tablespoons olive oil
½	teaspoon ground cumin
½	teaspoon salt
¼	teaspoon freshly ground pepper

▲ For the salad, bring the water to a boil in a medium saucepan. Stir in the couscous and salt. Return to a boil and remove from the heat. Let stand, covered, for 5 minutes. Spread on a tray to cool slightly, breaking up any lumps with a spoon.

▲ Combine the couscous with the tomatoes, green onions, celery, olives, parlsey and mint in a bowl.

▲ For the dressing, combine the lemon juice, olive oil, cumin and salt in a small jar. Cover and shake to mix well.

▲ Add the dressing to the salad and toss to coat well. Adjust the salt and add the pepper. Chill, covered, until serving time.

Just before the turn of the century, Elbridge Burbank, an Illinois painter, traveled throughout Indian territories in the West to paint Native Americans and document their lifestyles. In his book, Burbank Among the Indians, *he writes, 'The greatest Indian I have ever known was Chief Joseph, the Nez Perce—a soldier, statesman and gentleman by any standard.'*

ONE HUNDRED YEARS OF IDAHO ART

Warm Roasted Eggplant Salad with Bell Peppers and Tomatoes

serves eight

Ingredients

2	small firm eggplant
	Salt to taste
⅓	cup olive oil
4	ripe tomatoes
4	red, yellow or green bell peppers, roasted
1 to 2	tablespoons red wine vinegar
	Pepper to taste
1	tablespoon chopped fresh parsley or chives (optional)

This beautiful medley of roasted vegetables is very popular in Sicily where the dish originated. Omit the vinegar for an excellent appetizer.

▲ Cut the eggplant into ¼-inch slices. Sprinkle with salt in a colander or on a paper towel and let drain for 1 hour. Pat dry with paper towels. Brush both sides with some of the olive oil and place on a baking sheet. Cut the tomatoes crosswise into halves and place cut side up on the baking sheet.

▲ Broil until the eggplant slices are light golden brown on both sides and the tomato tops begin to brown. Cut the eggplant into narrow strips and the tomatoes into medium pieces. Peel and seed the roasted peppers and cut into thin strips. Combine with the eggplant and tomatoes in a bowl.

▲ Add the remaining olive oil, vinegar, salt and pepper and mix lightly. Sprinkle with the parsley. Serve warm or at room temperature.

Goose Creek Pear and Bleu Cheese Salad

serves eight

Shallot Vinaigrette

½   cup safflower oil
2   tablespoons red wine vinegar
2   tablespoons honey
1   tablespoon Dijon mustard
1   tablespoon water
1   shallot
⅛   teaspoon salt
¾   teaspoon pepper

Salad

1   head red leaf lettuce, torn
1   head Bibb lettuce, torn
2   pears, peeled, chopped
⅓   cup crumbled bleu cheese
⅓   cup pine nuts, toasted

This is a delicious and delightful flavor combination.

▲ For the vinaigrette, combine the oil, vinegar, honey, mustard, water, shallot, salt and pepper in a blender and process until smooth. Chill until serving time.

▲ For the salad, combine the leaf lettuce, Bibb lettuce, pears, bleu cheese and pine nuts in a bowl. Add the dressing and mix lightly. Serve immediately.

Provisioning processes were important for several reasons. Good health required good nutrition so what was preserved had to be well put up. Once snowed in, the family stayed in until perhaps April. To assure an adequate diet, at least the following supplies were stored: ten 50-pound sacks of flour stored in large tin cans; 100 pounds of white and 100 pounds of brown sugar; 100 pounds of rice; 5 gallons of honey; some sorghum; 5 or 10 pounds of baking powder; 15 gallons of kerosene…

IDAHO FOLKLIFE: HOMESTEADS TO HEADSTONES

Port and Stilton Salad

serves twelve

Port Dressing

½	cup olive oil
1	tablespoon walnut oil
1	tablespoon safflower oil
1	tablespoon lemon juice
1	tablespoon tarragon vinegar
3	tablespoons tawny port
1	tablespoon Dijon mustard
¼	teaspoon salt
¼	teaspoon pepper

Salad

1	clove of garlic
1½	tablespoons unsalted butter
2	teaspoons safflower oil
¾	cup walnuts
1	large head red leaf lettuce, torn
2	small heads Bibb lettuce, torn
2	Belgian endives, sliced
8	ounces Stilton cheese, crumbled

▲ For the dressing, combine the olive oil, walnut oil, safflower oil, lemon juice, vinegar, port, mustard, salt and pepper in a bowl and mix well.

▲ For the salad, sauté the garlic in the butter and safflower oil in a skillet for 2 minutes. Remove and discard the garlic. Add the walnuts to the skillet. Sauté until golden brown; drain.

▲ Toss the leaf lettuce and Bibb lettuce with half the dressing in a bowl. Toss the endives with the remaining dressing in a bowl. Combine with the walnuts and cheese in a serving bowl and toss lightly.

Elk, deer and mountain sheep were fairly common in the Nez Perce area, but trips were made across the mountains to obtain buffalo. The meat was either boiled or roasted, and was never partaken without some preparation. Bear meat was pit barbequed with fir boughs.

NATIVE FOODS USED BY THE NEZ PERCE INDIANS OF IDAHO

Spinach Salad with Chèvre and Roasted Shallots

serves four

Ingredients

⅔ cup light olive oil

⅓ cup extra-virgin olive oil

4 cloves of garlic, cut into quarters

4 bay leaves

1 tablespoon coarsely chopped fresh thyme

2 teaspoons dried basil

2 teaspoons coarsely chopped fresh rosemary

1 teaspoon peppercorns

12 ounces goat cheese, cut into 4 equal portions

1 pound medium shallots

½ cup balsamic vinegar

2 tablespoons water

1 tablespoon sugar

Salt and pepper to taste

1 (6-inch) sprig of rosemary

1 cup pecan halves

1 tablespoon vegetable oil

Salt to taste

1½ pounds tender spinach, trimmed

1 teaspoon finely chopped thyme

▲ Combine the olive oils, garlic, bay leaves, 1 tablespoon thyme, basil, chopped rosemary and peppercorns in a bowl and mix well. Add the cheese, coating well. Marinate, covered, in the refrigerator for 4 to 8 hours.

▲ Preheat the oven to 400 degrees. Remove the cheese to a plate.

▲ Strain the marinade into a 9x13-inch baking dish. Add the shallots, balsamic vinegar, water, sugar, salt, pepper and rosemary sprig. Bake, covered, for 55 minutes or until the shallots are tender.

▲ Discard the rosemary sprig. Strain the mixture into a nonreactive saucepan, reserving the shallots. Keep warm over very low heat.

▲ Toss the pecans with the vegetable oil and kosher salt in a bowl. Spread on a baking sheet. Bake for 7 minutes or until the pecans are toasted.

▲ Combine the cheese with the shallots in a baking dish. Bake for 3 minutes or just until heated through; do not melt the cheese.

▲ Mound the spinach on 4 individual plates. Place 1 portion of cheese on each plate. Drizzle with the dressing and sprinkle with the shallots, 1 teaspoon thyme and toasted pecans.

Sacajawea Tomato and Green Bean Salad

serves eight

Ingredients

8	ounces fresh green beans, trimmed
4	large beefsteak tomatoes
½	cup walnut oil or olive oil
½	cup raspberry vinegar
	Salt and pepper to taste
⅓	cup chopped walnuts
1	bunch fresh basil

▲ Blanch the green beans, drain and place in ice water. Cut the tomatoes into ¼-inch slices. Arrange the tomatoes and beans on a serving plate.

▲ Mix the walnut oil, vinegar, salt and pepper in a small bowl. Drizzle over the salad. Sprinkle with the walnuts and basil.

Clearwater Hot Chicken Salad

serves twelve

Ingredients

4	cups chopped cooked chicken
½	cup slivered almonds
2	cups finely chopped celery
1	cup shredded Cheddar cheese
2	cups mayonnaise
1 to 2	tablespoons lemon juice
1	teaspoon salt
	Pepper to taste
2	cups crushed potato chips
1	head lettuce

▲ Preheat the oven to 400 degrees.

▲ Combine the chicken, almonds, celery, cheese, mayonnaise, lemon juice, salt and pepper in a bowl and mix well.

▲ Spoon into a 9x13-inch baking dish and top with the potato chips. Bake for 10 minutes or just until heated through. Spoon onto lettuce-lined serving plates. Serve hot or cool.

Hells Canyon Chicken Salad

serves eight

Salad

1	pound bacon
5	large chicken breasts, cooked, cut into strips
1	large head lettuce, shredded
¾	cup chopped green onions
1	(3-ounce) can chow mein noodles
1	(8-ounce) can sliced water chestnuts, drained

Chicken Salad Dressing

⅓	cup vegetable oil
⅓	cup soy sauce
2	tablespoons honey
2	tablespoons ketchup
1	teaspoon dry mustard

This is a delightful summer salad.

▲ For the salad, cut the bacon into 1-inch pieces and fry in a skillet until crisp; drain. Combine with the chicken, lettuce, green onions, noodles and water chestnuts in a bowl and mix well. Chill until serving time.

▲ For the dressing, combine the oil, soy sauce, honey, ketchup and dry mustard in a bowl and mix well. Store in the refrigerator for up to 2 weeks.

▲ Add the dressing to the salad and toss to mix well.

The verse of advice of the 1930s depression period might well have applied to the early Idaho pioneers: 'Use it up, wear it out, make it do, or do without.'

FOOTPRINTS ON MOUNTAIN TRAILS

Cottonwood Butte Chicken Caesar Salad

serves eight

Caesar Salad Dressing

1	egg
½	teaspoon salt
3 to 4	cloves of garlic, crushed
1	teaspoon anchovy paste
1	tablespoon Dijon mustard
	Juice of ½ lemon
1	teaspoon Worcestershire sauce
1	teaspoon red wine vinegar
1	cup olive oil
½ to ⅓	cup grated Parmesan cheese

Salad

2	heads Romaine lettuce, sliced crosswise
4	chicken breasts, grilled, sliced
1	cup croutons

This is made with chicken, but turkey or other meat would also be good.

▲ For the dressing, cook the egg in boiling water in a saucepan for 1 minute and drain.

▲ Combine the salt, garlic, anchovy paste, mustard, egg, lemon juice, Worcestershire sauce and vinegar in a bowl in the order listed, mixing well after each addition. Add the olive oil gradually, whisking constantly to blend well. Stir in the cheese.

▲ For the salad, combine the lettuce with the dressing in a salad bowl and toss lightly. Top with the chicken and croutons.

When gold and silver were discovered in the north and central mountains of what is now Idaho in the 1860s, a surge of fortune seekers poured into the region...A small number of artists found their subject matter in the mining camps, and even though many works dating from the mid-nineteenth century have an amateur quality, they are important documents of western history...

ONE HUNDRED YEARS OF IDAHO ART

Curried Chicken Salad with Chutney and Grapes

serves six

Ingredients

4	cups chopped cooked chicken breasts
½	cup mango chutney
1½	cups chopped celery
2	tablespoons lemon juice
1	cup mayonnaise
2½	tablespoons soy sauce
1	tablespoon onion juice
2	teaspoons curry powder
½	cup toasted sliced almonds
½	cup sliced water chestnuts
1	cup green grapes
	Fresh fruit, carrot curls and/or black olives

This delicious salad was served at the Beaux Arts Spring Luncheon in 1993. It can easily be increased to serve a large group.

▲ Combine the chicken, chutney, celery, lemon juice, mayonnaise, soy sauce, onion juice and curry powder in a large bowl and mix well. Chill for 8 hours or longer.

▲ Add the almonds, water chestnuts and grapes and toss lightly. Garnish with fresh fruit, carrot curls and/or black olives.

"Spare time? Here in this canyon there is stock to be fed, wood to be split and brought in, dogs, cats and chickens to be fed, water holes to be chopped through the ice so four-legged ones can drink. There are floors to be swept, meals to be cooked, and dishes to wash. Laundry day is busy; both wash and rinse water must be heated. There are books to read, letters to write, trails to be shoveled clean after each snowfall. Before the mail plane can land, the runway must be snowshoe packed…Spare time? There is none."

Lydia Frances Coyle, Shoup, Idaho
IDAHO LONERS, HERMITS, SOLITARIES, AND INDIVIDUALISTS

Palouse Chicken Salad

serves eight

Chicken Salad Dressing

6	tablespoons fresh lime juice
¼	cup fish sauce (nuoc mam)
¼	cup packed light brown sugar
4	chiles, seeded, minced
	Nutmeg to taste
1	tablespoon chopped lemon grass
½	tablespoon grated fresh ginger
¼	cup chopped fresh mint
3	tablespoons minced fresh basil

Salad

3	cups vegetable oil
20	won ton skins, cut into ¼-inch strips
8	cups mixed salad greens
4	cups chopped roasted or grilled chicken
1	cup bean sprouts
1	large yellow bell pepper, julienned
1	European seedless cucumber, julienned
¼	cup dry-roasted unsalted peanuts, coarsely chopped

An unusual list of ingredients combine to make a delightful salad.

▲ For the dressing, combine the lime juice, fish sauce, brown sugar, chiles, nutmeg, lemon grass, ginger, mint and basil in a medium bowl and whisk until well mixed.

▲ For the salad, heat the oil in a large skillet over medium-high heat until a strip of won ton skips on the surface. Add the won ton strips in batches and fry for 1 minute or until crisp and golden brown, turning to brown evenly. Drain on paper towels.

▲ Combine the mixed greens, chicken, bean sprouts, bell pepper and cucumber in a large bowl. Add the dressing and toss lightly.

▲ Add the won tons and mix gently. Spoon onto a serving platter and top with the peanuts.

Whitewater Chicken and Pasta Salad

serves eight

Whitewater Dressing

1	cup fresh basil leaves
⅔	cup olive oil
	Juice of 1 lemon
1	clove of garlic, crushed
1	teaspoon Dijon mustard
¼	teaspoon salt
¼	teaspoon cayenne pepper

Salad

16	ounces uncooked rotelli
1	whole chicken breast, cooked, chopped
2	(7-ounce) jars marinated artichoke hearts, drained
1	(2-ounce) jar capers, drained
1	avocado, coarsely chopped
1	(4-ounce) jar green olives, drained, sliced
2	large tomatoes, peeled, seeded, coarsely chopped
4	green onions, chopped

▲ For the dressing, combine the basil, olive oil, lemon juice, garlic, mustard, salt and cayenne pepper in a food processor or blender and process until smooth.

▲ For the salad, cook the pasta al dente using the package directions; rinse in cold water and drain. Combine with the chicken, artichokes, capers, avocado, olives, tomatoes and green onions in a large bowl.

▲ Add the dressing and toss gently. Chill, covered, for 1 hour or longer.

China Creek Pork Salad

serves four

Ingredients

2	tablespoons olive oil
5	large (1½-inch) center-cut pork chops, very thinly sliced
2	cloves of garlic, minced
½	cup soy sauce
¼	cup rice vinegar
6	large carrots, julienned into 2-inch strips
½	teaspoon crushed red pepper
1	large red onion, thinly sliced
½	tablespoon sesame oil
1	head iceberg lettuce, torn

▲ Heat the olive oil to 425 degrees in a wok. Add the pork. Stir-fry for 3 to 4 minutes or until cooked through. Add the garlic and stir-fry for 1 minute.

▲ Add the soy sauce, rice vinegar, carrots and red pepper. Cook for 2 minutes. Reduce the wok heat to 300 degrees.

▲ Add the onion. Cook for 1 minute. Stir in the sesame oil.

▲ Arrange the lettuce on serving plates. Spoon the pork mixture over the lettuce. Garnish with mint leaves.

Large amounts of supplies had to be stored for winter use, as the snows were too deep and soft at times even for snowshoes…supply centers were always a long distance away, and creeks froze over, making it impossible to fish…

FOOTPRINTS ON MOUNTAIN TRAILS

River Rafters' Shrimp Summer Salad Platter
serves eight

Ingredients

¼	cup olive oil
½	tablespoon dry mustard
2	tablespoons balsamic vinegar
2	pounds frozen cooked jumbo prawns, thawed
2	tablespoons drained capers
1	(8-ounce) can black olives, drained
½	red onion, thinly sliced
½	red bell pepper, chopped
½	yellow bell pepper, chopped
2	tomatoes, chopped
	Juice of ½ lemon
½	lemon, thinly sliced
	Salt and pepper to taste

This can also be served as a refreshing first course or appetizer.

▲ Combine the olive oil, dry mustard and vinegar in a bowl and mix well. Add the shrimp and toss to coat well.

▲ Add the capers, olives, onion, bell peppers, tomatoes, lemon juice and sliced lemon and mix lightly. Season with salt and pepper.

▲ Chill, covered, or in a sealable plastic bag for several hours. Drain and arrange on a large platter with the lemon slices and olives on top.

Before 1860, Idaho was a wild, virtually unsettled region of varied terrain bisected by formidable mountains and the natural barriers of deep canyons and cascading rivers. For the majority of travelers, Idaho was not a destination, but a territory to be traversed on the way to the Pacific Coast.

ONE HUNDRED YEARS OF IDAHO ART

Salads

Shrimp and Pasta Salad with Oranges

serves four

Orange Vinaigrette

1	cup fresh orange juice
6	tablespoons olive oil
4	teaspoons balsamic vinegar
2½	tablespoons mixed fresh herbs, such as basil, mint or oregano
¾	teaspoon salt
⅛	teaspoon cayenne pepper

Salad

3	cups cooked orzo, about one cup uncooked
2	pounds uncooked large shrimp, peeled, deveined
2	tablespoons olive oil
	Salt and cayenne pepper to taste
2	heads green or red leaf lettuce, torn
5	bunches arugula or mixed greens with raddichio
½	cup minced fresh herbs, such as basil, mint or oregano
¼	red onion, thinly sliced
	Sections of 3 large oranges

▲ For the vinaigrette, whisk the orange juice, olive oil, vinegar, fresh herbs, salt and cayenne pepper in a bowl until smooth.

▲ For the salad, combine the pasta with 2½ tablespoons of the dressing in a bowl and toss to coat well; set aside.

▲ Sauté half the shrimp at a time in half the heated oil in a skillet over medium-high heat for 1 minute, sprinkling with salt and cayenne pepper.

▲ Combine the shrimp with ¼ cup of the vinaigrette in a bowl and mix well. Marinate for 20 to 30 minutes.

▲ Reserve ¼ cup of the remaining vinaigrette. Combine the lettuce, arugula, fresh herbs, onion and the remaining vinaigrette in a bowl and toss lightly. Spoon onto 4 serving plates.

▲ Place a mound of the pasta beside the greens. Arrange the shrimp and orange sections over the salad. Drizzle each with 1 tablespoon of the reserved vinaigrette.

Round-Up Summer Bread and Pasta Salad

serves six

Ingredients

4 to 6 slices country-style bread, crusts partially trimmed
¾ clove of garlic, minced
½ cup olive oil
6 to 12 tomatoes, peeled, seeded, chopped
1 cup chopped fresh basil
1 cup chopped fresh parsley
  Fresh thyme to taste
12 ounces pasta, cooked al dente, tossed with several drops of olive oil
  Salt and cracked pepper to taste

▲ Preheat the oven to 240 degrees.

▲ Process the bread into coarse crumbs in the food processor or blender. Measure 4 cups. Spread on a baking sheet. Bake until crisp and dry but not brown.

▲ Sauté the garlic in the hot olive oil in a skillet for 1 minute. Add the bread crumbs. Sauté until the crumbs are golden brown.

▲ Combine the tomatoes, basil, parsley and thyme in a bowl. Add the pasta and bread crumbs and toss lightly. Season with the salt and pepper. Garnish with additional basil and freshly ground pepper.

Life in the mining camps was especially hard for the women. Money was always a problem in those days—never enough of it. The women were, for the most part, severely limited in their education, for, as I have heard many times, "Women weren't supposed to know anything." The only work for women outside the home would be cooking for the large groups of men who worked the mines and lived in the boarding houses and/or washing their clothes.

FOOTPRINTS ON MOUNTAIN TRAILS

Gallery Three

Soups and Breads

Southwest Idaho

The mystic and legendary beauty of Payette Lake is as dramatic as it is serene. The glowing scene casts a spell and the expanse of shadows conjures up visions of wood-smoke and endless summer eves. People come to ski, they come to walk the alpine meadows and trails, they come to sail the glassy water or explore the cool, meandering streams.

Artists are dazzled by the possibilities.

"They say there is a land,
Where crystal waters flow,
O'er beds of quartz and purest gold,
Way out in Idaho…"

—*1800-Unknown*
WAY OUT IN IDAHO

McCall Fall Country Dinner

Packer John's Wild Game Potage, page 73
Syrah

or

German Goulash Soup, page 69
Lemberger

Payette Lake Baguettes, page 82

Red Cabbage Salad with Bacon and Goat Cheese, page 47

Apple-Blueberry Crispy Cobbler, page 206
or

Puffed Apple Tarts, page 219
Late Harvest Riesling

Idaho City Chicken and Bean Soup

serves four

Ingredients

1	cup chopped onion
1	tablespoon olive oil
2	(14-ounce) cans chicken broth
1	(16-ounce) can Great Northern or kidney beans
1	(4-ounce) can chopped green chiles
2	teaspoons dried oregano, crushed
1½	teaspoons ground cumin
1	teaspoon garlic powder
¼	teaspoon ground cloves
¼	teaspoon ground red pepper
3	cups chopped cooked chicken

This is so good you will want to double the recipe.

▲ Sauté the onion in the olive oil in a large kettle until translucent. Add the chicken broth.

▲ Rinse and drain the beans and add to the broth along with the green chiles, oregano, cumin, garlic powder, cloves and red pepper.

▲ Bring to a boil and then reduce heat. Cover and simmer for 20 minutes. Add the cooked chicken and continue to simmer, covered, for 10 minutes longer or until heated through. Ladle into soup bowls and garnish with shredded Monterey Jack cheese.

Mining was the magnet that attracted a wave of young men west, and with them came adventurous and hardy women. A pioneer Idaho City artist of note was Maggie F. Brown, who lived in the town from 1864 to 1882 at the height of the Idaho gold rush. Idaho City was a town of contrast, comprised of prospectors, Confederate refugees, and outlaws, as well as a local contingent of churchgoers and upright citizens. It was said that in Idaho City, "the priest and the saloon-keeper jostle each other on the sidewalks, and the gentleman's wife must walk around the trail of the courtesan who lives next door…"

ONE HUNDRED YEARS OF IDAHO ART

Payette River Chicken Bisque

serves four

Ingredients

1	(3-pound) chicken
3	tablespoons salt
4	stalks celery, cut into chunks
4	carrots, cut into chunks
2	onions, cut into quarters
4	quarts water
1	cup butter
1	cup flour
½	cup chopped pimentos
1	cup (or more) chopped cooked chicken
½	cup chopped green peppers, blanched
1	teaspoon MSG (optional)
½	teaspoon pepper
	Several drops of yellow food coloring

▲ Combine the chicken, salt, celery, carrots, onions and water in a large soup pot and bring to a boil. Cook until the chicken is tender and can easily be pulled off the bones. Bone the chicken; strain 8 cups of the chicken stock and reserve.

▲ Melt the butter in a heavy frying pan over medium heat. Stir in the flour. Cook for 20 minutes or until golden brown, stirring constantly.

▲ Bring the reserved chicken stock to a very low boil in a soup pot. Stir in the roux gradually. Simmer for 15 minutes or until the soup takes on a glaze. Add the pimentos, chicken, green peppers, MSG, pepper and food coloring. Cook until heated through. Serve immediately.

"When harvest time came the next summer, I stayed home while my husband went out to work the harvest fields. I was expecting my first baby in December, 1914 . . . it was so warm and rainless that the spring dried up and all I had was enough for the cooking and the chickens. Bending to necessity, I had to put the tub, washboard, and clothes on my saddlehorse and go over to Gibbs Creek to wash. The water there where the sun reached it was warm enough without heating it over a fire, and I hung the clothes on the bushes until they dried."

SALMON RIVER SAGA

German Goulash Soup

serves twelve

Ingredients

3	pounds chuck steak or roast, cubed
3	tablespoons vegetable oil
2 to 3	large cloves of garlic, minced
	Salt and pepper to taste
½	teaspoon garlic salt
1	teaspoon chili powder
1	teaspoon paprika
	Cayenne pepper to taste
2	(6-ounce) cans tomato paste
2	(6-ounce) cans water
2 to 3	large onions, chopped
2 to 3	large green peppers, chopped
½	cup chopped celery
3 to 4	potatoes, cubed (optional)
3 to 4	carrots, sliced (optional)
6	tablespoons flour
¼	cup water

This recipe is from a German cook in Bitburg, but it is reminiscent of good home cooking everywhere. It freezes well if the potatoes are omitted.

▲ Brown the cubed steak in the oil in a large soup pot. Add the minced garlic and season with salt, pepper, garlic salt, chili powder, paprika and cayenne pepper.

▲ Add the tomato paste and enough water to just cover the steak. Simmer for 1 hour. Add the onions, green peppers, celery and optional vegetables and stir to mix well. Do not add more water as vegetables will release liquid as they cook.

▲ Mix the flour and ¼ cup water to form a paste and stir into the soup. Simmer over low heat for 2½ hours. Adjust the seasonings.

The population of Idaho from its earliest days has been sparse. Artists who settled in Idaho towns received little outside visual or cultural stimulation...their works often acquired a naive quality after extended periods of living in cultural isolation. In addition, financial incentives for artists were lacking...and patronage was minimal...

ONE HUNDRED YEARS OF IDAHO ART

Garden Valley Chilled Pea Soup

serves eight

Ingredients

1	(10-ounce) package frozen peas
2	cups shredded lettuce
2	cups chicken broth
½	cup water
¼	cup tomato juice
¼	cup chopped green onions
1	tablespoon chopped fresh parsley
½	teaspoon salt
¼	teaspoon thyme
¼	teaspoon white pepper
1	cup whipping cream

▲ Combine the peas, lettuce, broth, water, tomato juice, green onions, parsley, salt, thyme and pepper in a large saucepan. Bring to a boil and cover. Reduce the heat and simmer for 20 minutes. Remove from heat and let cool.

▲ Process the pea mixture in a food processor until puréed. Stir in the whipping cream and chill until time to serve.

What we know of Idaho in its frontier years is greatly enhanced by the highly detailed views of early towns produced by itinerant artists. Edmond Greene made it his business to document mountains, scenic sites, mining districts and boom towns of southern Idaho. Although little is known of Edmond Greene personally, his renderings of Atlanta, Shoshone Falls, Bonanza City, Quartzburg, Garden Valley, and other sites remain an important record of pioneer Idaho.

ONE HUNDRED YEARS OF IDAHO ART

Ponderosa Tortilla Soup

serves four

Ingredients

1	cup finely chopped onion
1	tablespoon minced garlic
1	tablespoon olive oil
1	(16-ounce) can chopped tomatoes
1	(10-ounce) can tomato soup
1	(16-ounce) can beef or vegetable broth
1	(14-ounce) can chicken broth
1	cup water
1	teaspoon chili powder
1½	tablespoons Worcestershire sauce
2	tablespoons finely chopped jalapeño peppers
6	(6-inch) fresh corn tortillas
6	tablespoons sour cream
8	slices avocado
6	tablespoons shredded Cheddar cheese
2	tablespoons sliced black olives

Serve this delicious soup with cheese bread.

▲ Sauté the onion and garlic in the olive oil for 2 to 3 minutes. Add the tomatoes, soup, broths, water, chili powder, Worcestershire sauce and jalapeño peppers. Cook over medium heat for 20 minutes.

▲ Tear the tortillas into small strips and add to the soup. Cover and cook over medium-low heat for 20 to 25 minutes or until done to taste.

▲ Spoon the sour cream into 4 bowls. Top the sour cream with the avocado slices, cheese and olives. Ladle the soup into bowls and serve immediately.

Roasted Tomato Soup with Spinach Pesto

serves four

Soup

10	ripe plum tomatoes (about 1½ pounds)
5	tablespoons olive oil
2	cloves of garlic, minced
½	teaspoon dried oregano, crumbled
¼	teaspoon dried basil, crumbled
½	teaspoon freshly ground black pepper
½	cup finely chopped onion
1	cup chicken broth
¼	cup red burgundy
½	cup ricotta cheese
½	cup whipping cream
½	cup tomato paste
2	tablespoons freshly grated Parmesan cheese

Spinach Pesto

1	(10-ounce) package fresh spinach, washed, drained
¼	teaspoon salt
2	large cloves of garlic
1	tablespoon butter
6	ounces pine nuts
½	cup (about) grated Parmesan cheese
⅓	cup olive oil

The bright green pesto makes this excellent soup very attractive.

▲ For the soup, preheat the oven to 475 degrees. Cut the tomatoes lengthwise into halves and place cut side down in a large baking pan. Brush generously with 3 tablespoons of the oil and sprinkle with the garlic, oregano, basil and pepper. Roast the tomatoes for 15 to 20 minutes or until the edges are charred.

▲ Scrape the tomatoes, oil and herbs from the pan into a food processor and process until not quite smooth, leaving small chunks and charred black specks.

▲ Sauté the onion in the remaining 2 tablespoons oil in a saucepan until translucent. Whisk in the tomato purée, broth, wine, ricotta cheese, cream and tomato paste. Add the Parmesan cheese and taste, adding more pepper, basil and oregano if desired. Bring to a simmer.

▲ For the spinach pesto, purée the spinach, salt, garlic, butter, pine nuts and cheese in a food processor until smooth. Add the oil gradually, processing constantly until completely blended.

▲ Spoon the soup into serving bowls and top with the spinach pesto.

Packer John's Wild Game Potage

serves twelve

Ingredients

8	slices bacon, diced
2	onions, coarsely chopped
4	carrots, chopped
2	cups coarsely chopped celery
8	mushrooms, thickly sliced
1	clove of garlic, minced
8	cups homemade or low-sodium chicken broth
3	cups dry white wine
½	cup uncooked barley
½	teaspoon dried basil
½	teaspoon dried rosemary
½	teaspoon dried parsley
¼	teaspoon coarsely ground pepper
½	teaspoon salt
2	pheasant breasts, poached slightly, boned, coarsely chopped
4	dove breasts, poached slightly, boned, coarsely chopped

This hearty winter meal is a delicious way to use some of that game in the freezer. Serve it with warm, crusty French bread and a salad.

▲ Cook the bacon in a large Dutch oven, remove with slotted spoon and set aside. Sauté the onions, carrots, celery, mushrooms and garlic in the bacon drippings for 10 minutes or until tender.

▲ Add the cooked bacon, broth, wine, barley, basil, rosemary, parsley, pepper, salt, pheasant and dove breasts. Simmer, covered, for 1 to 2 hours.

John Welch, popularly known as Packer John, was a Lewiston miner who is said to have forged the trail that opened up Boise Basin to northern prospectors during the early days of Idaho's gold rush. In 1862, Welch constructed a rustic log cabin near New Meadows as a storehouse for his winter cache. The first meeting of the territorial Democratic convention took place here and was recorded by itinerant Idaho painter, U.L. Gray around 1910...

ONE HUNDRED YEARS OF IDAHO ART

Hill House Cinnamon Rolls

serves eighteen

Ingredients

1	envelope dry yeast
⅓	cup sugar
½	cup lukewarm water
½	cup milk, scalded, cooled to lukewarm
1	egg
¼	cup margarine, softened
½	teaspoon salt
3	cups unbleached flour, sifted
1½	pints whipping cream
¾ to 1	cup sugar
1	tablespoon (or more) cinnamon
1	teaspoon vanilla extract

Now closed, Hill House Restaurant was a Boise tradition. Sunday dinner was a highlight and the cinnamon rolls were one of the big attractions.

▲ Dissolve the yeast with 1 teaspoon of the sugar in the lukewarm water in a large bowl. Add the remaining ⅓ cup sugar, milk, egg, margarine and salt. Add 1 cup flour and mix with a fork to form a batter. Add the remaining flour, mixing to make a soft dough. Knead lightly on a floured surface and place in a greased bowl. Cover and let rise in a warm place for 2 hours or until doubled in bulk.

▲ Whip the cream in a mixer bowl until it begins to thicken. Add ¾ to 1 cup sugar, cinnamon and vanilla and continue whipping until soft peaks form. Cover and chill.

▲ Punch the dough down and separate into 3 equal portions. Roll each portion slightly more than ⅛ inch thick. Spread a small amount of the whipped cream mixture very thinly on the dough, spreading almost to the edges. Roll up tightly and slice rolls into ¾-inch pieces.

▲ Place the rolls cut side down with sides of rolls barely touching in a greased 11x16-inch baking pan with 3-inch sides. Cover and let rise for 1 to 2 hours or until doubled in bulk.

▲ Preheat the oven to 425 degrees. Spread the rolls with the remaining whipped cream mixture. Bake on the upper oven rack for 20 minutes or until done in the center. Invert to serve.

Sunshine Berry Coffee Cake

serves twelve

Coffee Cake

1	cup butter, softened
1	cup sugar
2	eggs
1	cup sour cream
1	teaspoon vanilla extract
2	cups flour
1	teaspoon baking powder
1	teaspoon baking soda
1	(21-ounce) can blueberry pie filling

Pecan Topping

¼	cup flour
¼	cup sugar
½	cup chopped pecans or walnuts
3	tablespoons butter

This was first made with huckleberry compote from the Priest Lake area. You may substitute 1½ to 2 cups fresh fruit compote for the pie filling used here.

▲ For the coffee cake, preheat the oven to 375 degrees and grease a 9x13-inch baking pan. Cream the butter and sugar in a mixer bowl until light and fluffy. Beat in the eggs 1 at a time. Stir in the sour cream and vanilla. Combine the flour, baking powder and baking soda in a bowl and gradually add to the butter mixture, beating well after each addition.

▲ For the topping, combine the flour, sugar and pecans in a bowl. Cut in the butter until mixture resembles coarse crumbs.

▲ Spread half the batter in the prepared pan. Top with the pie filling and then the remaining batter. Sprinkle with the topping.

▲ Bake for 45 minutes or until golden brown. Cut into squares to serve.

Wild onions were used for poultices, eaten fresh after exposure to high heat to reduce somewhat the potent odor of the fresh plant, and added to stews and beans. It is found almost everywhere in the mountains.

FOOTPRINTS ON MOUNTAIN TRAILS

Warm Lake Coffee Cakes

serves sixteen

Coffee Cake

2	envelopes dry yeast
½	cup warm water
⅓	cup butter or shortening
⅓	cup sugar
2	teaspoons salt
⅔	cup milk, scalded
2	eggs
5	cups (about) flour
1	cup chopped walnuts
1	cup sugar
2	teaspoons cinnamon

Coffee Cake Frosting

1	cup confectioners' sugar
3	tablespoons (about) milk

▲ For the coffee cake, dissolve the yeast in the warm water in a small bowl. Combine the butter, ⅓ cup sugar, salt and hot milk in a large bowl, stirring to melt the butter. Cool to lukewarm. Add the eggs and yeast mixture. Add enough flour to form a stiff dough.

▲ Knead on a lightly floured surface for 5 minutes and place in a greased bowl. Let rise until doubled in bulk.

▲ Mix the walnuts, 1 cup sugar and cinnamon in a small bowl.

▲ Preheat the oven to 350 degrees and grease two 10x15-inch baking pans.

▲ Divide the dough into halves. Roll one portion at a time to a 10x15-inch rectangle. Sprinkle each with half of the cinnamon mixture. Roll tightly as for a jelly roll starting with the long edge. Place in the prepared pan. Fold half of each roll on top of the other half and seal the ends together. Starting at the folded end, cut down the center with scissors to within 1 inch of the other end. Turn the cut halves flat to form a heart.

▲ Bake for 25 to 30 minutes or until golden brown.

▲ For the frosting, combine the confectioners' sugar with enough milk to make of the desired consistency in a bowl. Spread on the warm coffee cakes.

Winter Carnival Walnut-Topped Brunch Cake

serves ten

Ingredients

1	cup butter, softened
1¼	cups sugar
2	eggs
1	cup sour cream
2	cups flour
½	teaspoon baking soda
1½	teaspoons baking powder
	Salt to taste
¾	cup chopped walnuts
1	teaspoon cinnamon
2	tablespoons sugar

▲ Cream the butter and 1¼ cups sugar in a mixer bowl until light and fluffy. Blend in the eggs and sour cream. Combine the flour, baking soda, baking powder and salt in a bowl and add to the butter mixture, mixing well. Spoon half the batter into a greased and floured bundt pan.

▲ Combine the walnuts, cinnamon and 2 tablespoons sugar in a small bowl. Sprinkle over the batter and top with the remaining batter. Place in a cold oven and set the oven temperature at 350 degrees. Bake for 50 to 55 minutes or until the top springs back when lightly touched. Remove to a wire rack to cool.

"By the time I was eight years old, I had become inseparably associated with our kitchen range. It was my job to keep the wood box beside it filled and the kindling supply replenished, and to carry out the ashes weekly or oftener. I kept these jobs until I went off to college. The wood stocking turned out to be an education in itself…but the skills I learned are almost as much abandoned now as the region where I learned it."

SALMON RIVER SAGA

Horseshoe Bend Angel Biscuits

serves twenty-four

Ingredients

2   envelopes dry yeast
2   tablespoons sugar
3   tablespoons lukewarm water
5   cups flour
1   teaspoon baking soda
3½   teaspoons baking powder
1½   teaspoons salt
1   cup shortening
2   cups buttermilk, slightly warmed
2   tablespoons melted butter

▲ Dissolve the yeast and sugar in the lukewarm water in a small bowl. Combine the flour, baking soda, baking powder and salt in a large bowl. Cut in the shortening with a pastry blender. Add the buttermilk and yeast mixture, stirring just until blended.

▲ Knead on a lightly floured surface until smooth. Roll ½ inch thick and cut into circles. Place fairly close together on an ungreased baking pan. Let rise for 1½ hours.

▲ Preheat the oven to 400 degrees. Brush the biscuits with the melted butter. Bake for 12 to 15 minutes or until the tops are lightly browned.

Brundage Sweet Corn Bread

serves twelve

Ingredients

1   cup cornmeal
2   cups flour
1   tablespoon baking powder
½   teaspoon salt
1½   cups sugar
4   large egg yolks
1   cup half-and-half
1   teaspoon vanilla extract
¾   cup melted butter
4   large egg whites

▲ Preheat the oven to 350 degrees and grease a 9x13-inch baking dish. Combine the cornmeal, flour, baking powder, salt and sugar in a large bowl. Combine the egg yolks, half-and-half, vanilla and melted butter in a small bowl. Add to the dry ingredients and mix well.

▲ Beat the egg whites until stiff and fold gently into the batter. Pour into the prepared dish.

▲ Bake for 30 minutes or until the top is golden brown and the center springs back when lightly touched.

Turn-of-the-Century Waffles
serves four

Ingredients

3	egg yolks
2	cups buttermilk
2	cups flour
2	teaspoons baking powder
1	teaspoon baking soda
¼	teaspoon salt
6	tablespoons vegetable oil
3	egg whites

This delicious recipe has been enjoyed by three generations.

▲ Beat the egg yolks in a bowl. Add the buttermilk, flour, baking powder, baking soda and salt and mix well. Beat in the oil.

▲ Beat the egg whites in a mixer bowl until stiff peaks form. Fold into the batter.

▲ Bake in a waffle iron using the manufacturer's directions.

TRAIL BREAD: Sometimes the bread will burn and the center will be raw. You can avoid this by setting the dough to rise at night, and in the morning, fry it in small cakes in a pan. Turn it often to keep it from burning. If mosquitoes are thick, they can get into the dough and turn it black. There is nothing you can do about this.

Kathryn Troxel - Food of the Overland Immigrants
WOMEN'S VOICES FROM THE OREGON TRAIL

Cascade Banana Bread

serves eight

Ingredients

1¾	cups flour
⅔	cup sugar
2	teaspoons baking powder
½	teaspoon baking soda
¼	teaspoon salt
1	cup mashed bananas
⅓	cup applesauce
2	tablespoons milk
2	eggs or equivalent egg substitute
¼	cup nuts (optional)

This is a low-fat recipe.

▲ Preheat the oven to 350 degrees and grease a loaf pan.

▲ Combine 1 cup of the flour with the sugar, baking powder, baking soda and salt in a large bowl. Add the bananas, applesauce and milk, stirring to mix well. Blend in the eggs and remaining flour. Stir in the nuts.

▲ Spoon into the prepared loaf pan. Bake for 55 to 60 minutes or until a wooden pick inserted in the center comes out clean. Cool for 10 minutes before inverting onto a wire rack to cool.

Sometimes when baking powder was available, the same procedure was followed. A depression was made in the flour, a little baking powder and salt were added, as was some bacon grease and water. This was mixed into a soft dough and wrapped around a stick and baked.

FOOTPRINTS ON MOUNTAIN TRAILS

Long Valley Oatmeal Carrot Bread

serves eight

Bread

1	cup quick-cooking or rolled oats
½	cup skim milk
2½	cups flour
1	cup packed brown sugar
1	tablespoon baking powder
½	teaspoon baking soda
½	teaspoon cinnamon
¼	teaspoon salt
1½	cups shredded carrots
½	cup raisins
1	(8-ounce) can juice-pack crushed pineapple
4	egg whites or 2 whole eggs
¼	cup vegetable oil
1	teaspoon vanilla extract

Cream Cheese Spread

4	ounces light cream cheese, softened
2	teaspoons brown sugar
¼	teaspoon vanilla extract

▲ For the bread, preheat the oven to 350 degrees and lightly spray the bottom of a loaf pan with nonstick cooking spray. Combine the oats and milk in a medium bowl and set aside.

▲ Mix the flour, brown sugar, baking powder, baking soda, cinnamon and salt in a large bowl. Stir in the carrots and raisins. Add the undrained pineapple, eggs, oil and vanilla to the oat mixture, mixing well. Add the oat mixture to the dry ingredients, stirring just until moistened.

▲ Spoon into the prepared pan. Bake for 60 to 75 minutes or until a wooden pick inserted in the center comes out clean and the crust is golden brown. Cool in the pan for 10 minutes and remove to a wire rack to cool completely.

▲ For the cream cheese spread, beat the cream cheese, brown sugar and vanilla in a bowl until smooth. Serve with the bread. Store, covered, in the refrigerator for up to 3 days.

Payette Lake Baguettes

serves eight

Ingredients

1	envelope dry yeast
2	cups lukewarm water
1	tablespoon sugar
2	teaspoons salt
4 to 5	cups flour
1	egg
1	tablespoon water

▲ Dissolve the yeast in 2 cups lukewarm water in a large bowl. Add the sugar and salt. Let stand for 10 minutes. Stir in about 4 cups of the flour to form a soft dough.

▲ Place on a floured surface. Use a pastry scraper or large spatula to lift and turn dough until it is firm enough to knead. Knead for 10 minutes or until smooth and elastic, adding additional flour as needed. Place in a warm bowl and cover with plastic wrap. Let rise in a warm place for 45 minutes. You may use an oven which has been preheated to 140 degrees and then turned off.

▲ Scrape the side of the bowl with a rubber spatula to loosen dough and remove to a lightly floured surface. Pat flat, dust with a small amount of flour, and fold in half to form a half circle, then in half again to form a quarter circle. Return to the bowl and let rise for 30 minutes longer.

▲ Pat the dough flat on a lightly floured surface. Fold in half. Cut into 4 equal portions, shape into balls and let rest for 5 minutes. Flatten each ball into an oval and roll to form a loaf, rolling back and forth until almost the length of the baguette pan.

▲ Place in baguette pans lined with pastry cloths. Cover with a clean cloth and let rise until nearly doubled in bulk.

▲ Preheat the oven to 450 degrees. Slide the loaves out of the pans by the bottom cloths. Brush the pans with melted butter. Gently roll the loaves back onto the pans using the cloths.

▲ Beat the egg and water together and brush onto the loaves. Slash the loaves diagonally about ¼ inch deep with a thin sharp knife. Bake for 20 to 25 minutes or until golden brown.

Mrs. Hofstetter's Potato Bread

serves thirty-six

Ingredients

8	russet potatoes
	Salt to taste
8	cups water
3	tablespoons yeast
3	tablespoons salt
20	(or more) cups flour (5 pounds)

Mrs. Hofstetter is from Switzerland and lives in Picabo, Idaho. She bakes these loaves at higher heat for the first 15 minutes to almost blacken the bottom crust. You might experiment to get the crust you like. They freeze well and taste great toasted.

▲ Boil the potatoes in salted water to cover in a covered saucepan until tender. Cool, peel, and grate into a very large bowl.

▲ Heat 8 cups of water in a saucepan and blend into the grated potatoes to form a mush; some lumps should remain. Cool until the mixture feels warm on your wrist.

▲ Add the yeast and salt and mix well. Add enough flour to form a stiff dough. Cover and let rise in a warm place until doubled in bulk.

▲ Knead on a lightly floured surface until smooth and elastic, kneading in additional flour if needed. Shape into 6 loaves the size of French bread loaves. Make shallow, diagonal cuts in the tops. Place on a baking sheet. Cover and let rise again until doubled in bulk.

▲ Preheat the oven to 350 degrees. Bake the loaves for 50 minutes.

Featherville Quick Loaf Bread

serves twelve

Ingredients

2	envelopes dry yeast
2⅔	cups (105- to 115-degree) water
2	teaspoons sugar
2	teaspoons salt
7	cups (about) bread flour or all-purpose flour

This recipe makes great bread with very little effort. Leftover bread will keep well for several days if wrapped in plastic wrap.

▲ Dissolve the yeast in the water in a large bowl. Add the sugar, stir, and let stand for 5 to 10 minutes or until foamy. Add the salt and 3 cups of the flour, beating until smooth.

▲ Add just enough of the remaining flour 1 cup at a time to form a soft dough. Knead on a lightly floured surface for 2 minutes. Place in a greased bowl and turn dough to coat the surface. Cover and let rise in a warm place for 30 minutes or until doubled in bulk.

▲ Punch dough down and divide into halves. Shape into 2 loaves and place in greased loaf pans. Cover and let rise for 30 minutes or until doubled in bulk.

▲ Preheat the oven to 400 degrees. Bake for 30 minutes or until the tops are brown and the loaves sound hollow when tapped. Remove to a wire rack to cool.

FRIED CAKES . . . . Take a little flour and water and make some dough, roll it thin, cut it into square blocks, then take some beef fat and fry them. You need not put either salt or pearl ash in your dough.

WOMEN'S VOICES FROM THE OREGON TRAIL

Whitewater Kranz

serves nine

Sweet Bread

1	cup milk
1	envelope dry yeast
¼	cup butter, softened
⅓	cup sugar
2	eggs, at room temperature
3	cups flour
	Salt to taste
2	tablespoons butter, softened
⅓	cup raisins
1 or 2	tablespoons finely chopped citron
¼	cup sugar
1	teaspoon cinnamon
⅓	cup toasted slivered almonds

Kranz Frosting

1	cup confectioner's sugar
½	teaspoon vanilla extract
2 to 3	tablespoons milk

▲ For the sweet bread, heat the milk in a saucepan to 105 to 115 degrees or until it feels comfortably warm on the wrist. Dissolve the yeast in the warm milk and set aside.

▲ Cream the butter and ⅓ cup sugar in a large bowl until light and fluffy. Beat in the eggs. Mix the flour and salt together. Add to the creamed mixture alternately with the yeast mixture, mixing well after each addition. Cover the bowl and let rise in a warm place for 8 hours or until doubled in bulk.

▲ Roll into a rectangle on a floured surface. Spread with 2 tablespoons butter and sprinkle with the raisins and citron. Combine ¼ cup sugar and cinnamon and sprinkle on top. Cut the rectangle into halves lengthwise. Roll each piece tightly from the long edge and twist to form a circle, sealing the seam. Place in 2 buttered 9-inch baking pans, placing a small buttered glass baking dish or custard cup in the center of each pan. Cover and let rise again until doubled in bulk.

▲ Preheat the oven to 350 degrees. Bake for 15 to 20 minutes or until golden brown. Remove to a wire rack to cool slightly.

▲ For the frosting, combine the confectioners' sugar with the vanilla and enough milk to make a stiff frosting. Spread on the warm bread. Sprinkle with the almonds.

Gallery Four

Side Dishes and Pasta

South Idaho

The great Snake River runs for 800 miles through
Southern Idaho with tributaries carving craggy, mahogany
canyons. Sheer walls rise to meet blue grey deserts of sage and
birds of prey nest in peace. Southern Idaho was the last of the
United States to be seen by eastern explorers. Lewis & Clark
came in 1805, followed by fur traders in 1808 and Oregon
Trail pioneers in 1843. The call of gold and silver was next,
and word about Idaho spread like wildfire.

*"Pure air, abundant water, a climate suited to the production of all the
fruits, vegetables, and cereals known to the temperate zone will surely soon be
appreciated and this favored territory be the point to which the expectant eyes
will turn."*

IDAHO TERRITORY 1881

Summer Picnic at Ste. Chapelle's Winery

Bonner's Ferry Smoked Turkey in Pumpkin Biscuits, page 23

Chicken and Shrimp Satay with Peanut Sauce, page 20

Cataldo Mission Vegetarian Pizza Delight, page 27

Tomatoes with Balsamic Vinegar and Provolone, page 97

Chocolate Chip Cookies with Walnuts and Raisins, page 203

Sheepherder's Chocolate Cake, page 198

Chardonnay–Fumé Blanc

Baked Vegetables Provençal

serves four

Ingredients

2	tablespoons olive oil
1	large eggplant
1	large red bell pepper
1	medium onion
2	large plum tomatoes, coarsely chopped
2	tablespoons white wine vinegar or 2 tablespoons red wine vinegar
2	tablespoons olive oil
	Salt and pepper to taste
¼	cup chopped fresh Italian parsley (cilantro)
8	Niçoise olives (optional)

This beautiful medley of roasted vegetables is very popular in Sicily where the dish originated. It can be prepared a day in advance and refrigerated. Simply stir and garnish when ready to serve.

▲ Preheat the oven to 350 degrees and pour 2 tablespoons oil into a 10x15-inch baking pan.

▲ Cut the eggplant, red pepper and onion into halves lengthwise. Trim the eggplant and remove the pepper seeds. Lay the vegetables cut side down in the prepared pan. Bake for 40 minutes or until the eggplant is very tender. Cool briefly and peel the eggplant.

▲ Chop the baked vegetables coarsely and place in a strainer with the tomatoes; press gently to remove the excess liquid. Combine with the vinegar, remaining oil, salt and pepper in a bowl and mix lightly. Top with the parsley and olives before serving.

▲ For an excellent appetizer, omit the vinegar and serve with fresh crusty bread.

Sioux, Cheyenne, gold camps, gambling rooms, dance halls, …Idaho, Placerville, Orofino, Boise Basin, Silver City, excitement, adventure, danger, hardship, toil. Gain, loss, love, life—the bright panorama flitted desultorily across the screen of memory, its flashes and pauses only partly answerable to the will…

SALMON RIVER SAGA

Green Beans with Balsamic-Glazed Onions

serves ten

Balsamic-Glazed Onions

2	pounds fresh pearl onions or 2 (16-ounce) packages frozen pearl onions, thawed
¼	cup balsamic vinegar
2	tablespoons unsalted butter
2	tablespoons vegetable oil
2	teaspoons chopped fresh thyme or 1 teaspoon dried thyme
1	teaspoon freshly ground pepper
½	teaspoon salt

Beans

3	pounds fresh green beans, trimmed
	Salt to taste
¼	cup mild olive oil
1	tablespoon Dijon mustard
¼	cup balsamic vinegar
½	teaspoon salt
½	teaspoon pepper

The natural sugar in balsamic vinegar caramelizes the pearl onions with a dark glaze and adds a touch of sweetness to the mustard-vinegar sauce.

▲ For the onions, combine the onions with boiling water in a saucepan and blanch for 1 minute. Drain and rinse with cold water. Peel and trim the onions.

▲ Combine the balsamic vinegar, butter, oil, thyme, pepper and salt in a small, nonreactive saucepan. Cook over medium-low heat until the butter is melted. Combine with the onions in a medium bowl and mix to coat well. Spread in a single layer on a baking sheet.

▲ Preheat the oven to 400 degrees. Roast the onions for 35 to 40 minutes or until evenly browned, stirring frequently. Remove and set aside. Reduce the oven temperature to 350 degrees.

▲ For the beans, combine the green beans with salted boiling water in a large saucepan and blanch for 4 minutes or until tender-crisp. Rinse with cold water and drain.

▲ Combine the olive oil, mustard, balsamic vinegar, ½ teaspoon salt and pepper in a large bowl. Add the beans and onions, toss well and transfer to a casserole. Cover and bake for 20 minutes or until heated through.

Green Beans Caesar

serves eight

Ingredients

2	pounds green beans, trimmed
1	cup minced green onions
½	cup minced celery
1	clove of garlic, minced
2	tablespoons butter
½	cup minced parsley
½	teaspoon each basil and rosemary
1½	teaspoons salt

▲ Cook the beans in water to cover in a saucepan for 12 minutes or until tender.

▲ Sauté the green onions, celery and garlic in the butter in a skillet for 5 minutes. Add the parsley, basil, rosemary and salt. Simmer, covered, over low heat for several minutes.

▲ Drain the beans and add to the skillet, mixing lightly. Cook until heated through. Garnish with cheese croutons.

Sautéed Green Beans with Radishes

serves eight

Ingredients

1	pound green beans, trimmed
2	teaspoons fennel seeds
1	tablespoon olive oil
1	tablespoon butter
4	ounces radishes, sliced
3 or 4	green onions, sliced
1	tablespoon lemon juice
¼	teaspoon salt
	Pepper to taste

▲ Cook the beans in water to cover in a saucepan for 4 minutes. Rinse with cold water and drain.

▲ Sauté the fennel seeds and beans in the heated olive oil and butter in a large skillet for 3 minutes, stirring frequently. Add the radishes, green onions, lemon juice, salt and pepper. Sauté until the beans are tender-crisp and heated through. Serve immediately.

Broccoli with Pine Nuts and Raisins

serves six

Ingredients

1	bunch broccoli
1	dried red pepper, crushed
2	cloves of garlic, slivered
¼	cup olive oil
½	cup pine nuts
½	cup raisins
2	large tomatoes, chopped
	Salt and pepper to taste

Great for buffets or picnics, this can be made in advance and stored in the refrigerator; let it return to room temperature to serve.

▲ Cut the broccoli into florets; trim and peel the stems and cut into thin slices.

▲ Sauté the red pepper and garlic in the heated olive oil in a skillet. Add the pine nuts and raisins and sauté for 2 minutes or just until the pine nuts begin to brown. Add the broccoli and sauté for 5 minutes longer.

▲ Add the tomatoes. Cook for 1 minute or just until heated through. Season with salt and pepper. Serve at room temperature.

"When spring arrived, we put in a garden. The ground had black soil and was sub-irrigated, so everything we planted produced in abundance. I dried corn and my husband piled up bean vines around a stake and threshed them out when dry. We had potatoes, tomatoes, watermelons, squash, onions, lettuce, ground cherries, turnips and peas. I canned a lot of vegetables that summer."

SALMON RIVER SAGA

Side Dishes
Warm Springs Carrots and Grapes
serves six

Ingredients

1½	pounds carrots, sliced
1	cup orange juice
¼	cup sugar
2	tablespoons white wine
¼	cup cornstarch
¼	cup water
1	small bunch seedless grapes

▲ Parboil the carrots until tender-crisp and chill in ice water. Drain and set aside.

▲ Combine the orange juice, sugar and wine in a saucepan and bring to a boil. Combine the cornstarch and water in a small bowl and whisk into the orange juice mixture.

▲ Cook until clear and thickened, stirring constantly. Add the carrots and grapes and cook until heated through. Serve immediately.

Side Dishes
Sautéed Carrots
serves eight

Ingredients

⅔	cup minced red onion
1	teaspoon Dijon mustard
1	tablespoon white wine vinegar
	Salt and pepper to taste
6	tablespoons vegetable oil
1	pound carrots, grated
4	teaspoons fresh mint or 2 teaspoons dried mint
¼	cup white wine vinegar
1	bunch watercress, chopped

▲ Combine the onion with water to cover in a bowl; let stand for several minutes. Mix the mustard, 1 tablespoon vinegar, salt, pepper and 2 tablespoons of the oil in a bowl.

▲ Sauté the carrots in the remaining 4 tablespoons oil in a large skillet until light brown. Add the mint and cook for several minutes. Remove from the heat. Stir in ¼ cup vinegar, salt and pepper. Cool to room temperature.

▲ Drain the onion and add to the carrots with the mustard mixture and watercress; toss lightly to coat well.

Jordan Valley Jalapeño Corn Casserole

serves nine

Ingredients

1½	cups cream-style corn
1	cup yellow cornmeal
½	teaspoon baking soda
1	cup melted butter
¾	cup buttermilk
2	medium onions, chopped
2	eggs, beaten
2	cups shredded sharp Cheddar cheese
4	fresh or canned jalapeño peppers, seeded, finely chopped

This casserole may be prepared in advance and reheated to serve. Substitute a small can of chopped mild chile peppers for the jalapeños if this version is too spicy.

▲ Preheat the oven to 350 degrees.

▲ Combine the corn, cornmeal, baking soda, butter, buttermilk, onions and eggs in a bowl and mix well. Pour half the batter into a greased 9x9-inch baking pan and cover with half the cheese. Sprinkle with the peppers and remaining cheese. Top with the remaining batter. Bake for 1 hour. Cool for 15 minutes and cut into squares.

"During World War I we were rationed. We had to use mixed flour with the white flour. I made some of it into steamed brown bread with raisins and molasses. It was hard to do much fruit canning because of the little amount of sugar received. I remember potatoes were very scarce that spring. My husband planted a hundred pounds of them. They were treated with something, and never came up. We had potatoes one meal a day, and turnips the other ones."

SALMON RIVER SAGA

Gold Rush Burgundy Mushrooms

serves sixteen

Ingredients

1½	cups butter
1	quart burgundy
2	tablespoons Worcestershire sauce
1	teaspoon dillseeds or ¾ teaspoon dillweed
1	teaspoon pepper
1	teaspoon garlic powder
2	cups boiling water
3	beef bouillon cubes
4	pounds mushrooms

This is an excellent party dish.

▲ Combine the butter, wine, Worcestershire sauce, dill, pepper, garlic powder, boiling water and bouillon cubes in a large Dutch oven and bring to a boil.

▲ Add the mushrooms and reduce heat to a simmer. Simmer, covered, for 5 hours. Simmer, uncovered, for 4 hours longer or until the liquid just covers the mushrooms.

Spicy Glazed Onions

serves eight

Ingredients

6	large onions
6	tablespoons butter
1	cup Madeira
¼	cup chopped parsley
	Salt and pepper to taste

▲ Slice the onions ¼ inch thick. Toss lightly in the heated butter in a skillet for 1 minute or just until coated; do not cook until tender. Add ⅔ cup of the wine.

▲ Cook, covered, for 5 minutes or until tender. Cook, uncovered, until the liquid is reduced to a glaze.

▲ Add the remaining wine, parsley, salt and pepper. Cook just until heated through.

Braised Peas with Lettuce

serves eight

Ingredients

2	(16-ounce) packages frozen tiny peas
24	pearl onions, blanched
4	lettuce leaves, shredded
½	cup chicken stock
½	cup melted butter
	Salt and pepper to taste
2	tablespoons sugar

▲ Combine the peas, onions, lettuce and chicken stock with the melted butter in a heavy saucepan. Season with salt and pepper.

▲ Simmer, covered, for 5 minutes. Add the sugar and simmer for 4 minutes longer.

Minted Peas in Tomato Cups

serves eight

Ingredients

8	small to medium tomatoes
1	(16-ounce) package frozen tiny peas, thawed
3	tablespoons chopped fresh mint
3	tablespoons melted butter or margarine
	Salt and pepper to taste

Here's a beautiful vegetable dish with no last-minute work.

▲ Preheat the oven to 375 degrees.

▲ Slice ¼ inch from the top of each tomato and scoop out the pulp; invert the shells on paper towels to drain.

▲ Combine the peas, mint, butter, salt and pepper in a bowl. Spoon about 3 tablespoons of the mixture into each tomato shell. Place in a shallow baking dish. Bake, covered, for 15 minutes or until heated through.

Tomatoes with Balsamic Vinegar and Provolone
serves four

Ingredients

4	large beefsteak tomatoes
2	tablespoons extra-virgin olive oil
½	cup balsamic vinegar
	Pepper to taste
1	clove of garlic, minced
3	basil leaves, minced
8	ounces extra-sharp provolone cheese, shredded
2	whole basil leaves

A crusty loaf of Italian bread goes well with this.

▲ Chop the tomatoes into bite-size chunks and place in a large serving dish. Combine the oil, vinegar, pepper, garlic, and minced basil in a small bowl and mix well. Pour over the tomatoes and toss to coat well.

▲ Sprinkle with the cheese and top with the whole basil leaves. Serve at room temperature.

Bogus Basin Broiled Tomatoes with Sherry
serves eight

Ingredients

4	large firm ripe tomatoes
¼	cup dry sherry
½	teaspoon salt
¼	teaspoon pepper
1	teaspoon dried oregano
½	cup mayonnaise
¼	cup grated Parmesan cheese

These tomatoes are delicious and go well with almost anything, especially beef or lamb chops.

▲ Preheat the oven to 300 degrees.

▲ Cut the tomatoes into halves and place cut side up in a shallow baking dish; prick with a fork. Sprinkle with the sherry and let stand for several minutes. Sprinkle with the salt, pepper and oregano.

▲ Bake for 5 minutes. Top with the mayonnaise and cheese. Broil until light brown. Serve immediately.

Breakfast Soufflé

serves six

Ingredients

8	large croissants
12	eggs
1½	cups half-and-half
2	cups shredded Cheddar cheese
½	teaspoon dry mustard
½	teaspoon garlic and herb seasoning blend
8	ounces bacon, crisp-fried, crumbled

▲ Tear the croissants into small pieces and spread evenly in a buttered 9x13-inch baking dish. Beat the eggs lightly in a large bowl and add the half-and-half, Cheddar cheese, dry mustard and seasoning blend, mixing well. Pour over the croissants, cover with plastic wrap and refrigerate for 8 hours or longer.

▲ Preheat the oven to 325 degrees. Remove the plastic wrap and sprinkle with the bacon. Bake for 45 to 60 minutes or until puffed and golden brown. Serve immediately.

Eggs Fantastic

serves six

Ingredients

12	ounces bulk breakfast sausage, crumbled
4	ounces mushrooms, sliced
1	medium onion, chopped
	Salt and pepper to taste
6	eggs
3	tablespoons sour cream
¼	cup Mexican salsa
8	ounces Velveeta cheese
8	ounces medium Cheddar cheese
8	ounces mozzarella cheese, sliced

▲ Preheat the oven to 400 degrees and butter a 7x11-inch baking dish.

▲ Brown the sausage with the mushrooms, onion, salt and pepper in a skillet, stirring until the sausage is crumbly. Drain well on paper towels.

▲ Combine the eggs and sour cream in a blender and process for 1 minute. Pour into the baking dish and bake for 8 to 10 minutes or until set in the middle. Reduce the oven temperature to 300 degrees.

▲ Layer the salsa, sausage mixture, Velveeta cheese, Cheddar cheese and mozzarella cheese over the eggs. Bake, uncovered, for 45 minutes. Let stand for 5 to 10 minutes before serving.

Side Dishes

Birds of Prey Fruit Compote

serves twelve

Ingredients

2	(12-ounce) packages mixed pitted dried fruits
2	(21-ounce) cans juice-pack pineapple chunks
2	(21-ounce) cans cherry pie filling
1	cup dry sherry
1	tablespoon curry powder

This is an easy recipe that is great with ham for a party.

▲ Preheat the oven to 350 degrees. Cut the large pieces of dried fruit into halves. Combine with the undrained pineapple, pie filling, sherry and curry powder in a 3-quart casserole.

▲ Bake, covered, for 30 minutes. Bake, uncovered, for 45 minutes longer. Let stand for 45 minutes or longer before serving.

Cranberry Sauce with Mint Garnish

serves ten

Ingredients

1	cup water
½	cup sugar
½	cup packed brown sugar
1	(12-ounce) package fresh or frozen cranberries
3	tablespoons prepared horseradish
1	tablespoon Dijon mustard
3	sprigs of mint (optional)

Serve this sauce with turkey, beef or pork, or spoon over cream cheese and serve with crackers.

▲ Combine the water, sugar and brown sugar in a medium saucepan, stirring well. Bring to a boil over medium heat and add the cranberries. Return to a boil and cook for 10 minutes, stirring occasionally. Spoon into a bowl and cool to room temperature.

▲ Stir in the horseradish and mustard. Chill, covered, until serving time. Garnish with the mint sprigs.

Hull's Gulch Potatoes Boulangerie

serves four

Ingredients

2	medium onions, thinly sliced
1	tablespoon vegetable oil
3	tablespoons butter
4	large potatoes, peeled and thinly sliced
	Salt and pepper to taste
	Fresh or dried rosemary to taste

▲ Preheat the oven to 375 degrees and butter a 2-quart baking dish.

▲ Sauté the onions in the oil and butter in a skillet until tender. Drain and reserve the liquid.

▲ Alternate layers of potatoes and onions in the baking dish, seasoning the layers with salt, pepper and rosemary. Pour the reserved liquid into the baking dish and add just enough water to cover.

▲ Bake for 40 minutes or until the potatoes are cooked through.

Boise River Festival Potato Strata

serves eight

Ingredients

6	large potatoes, peeled, cut into halves
	Salt to taste
6	green onions, chopped
2	cups shredded Cheddar cheese
1	(10-ounce) can cream of mushroom soup
2	cups sour cream
½	cup melted butter
1	cup crushed potato chips

This is wonderful with grilled steak. It can also be made ahead and frozen; thaw before baking.

▲ Preheat the oven to 350 degrees and butter a large baking dish. Parboil the potatoes in salted boiling water in a saucepan for 15 to 20 minutes only. Drain and set aside to cool.

▲ Combine the green onions, cheese, soup, sour cream and butter in a large bowl. Grate the potatoes into the bowl and mix well. Spoon into the prepared dish and top with the potato chips. Bake for 45 minutes or until golden brown and bubbling.

Owyhees Crab-Stuffed Potatoes

serves eight

Ingredients

4	large baking potatoes
1	tablespoon butter or shortening
½	cup melted butter
½	cup heavy cream
1	teaspoon salt
⅛	teaspoon cayenne pepper
4	teaspoons grated onion
1	cup shredded sharp Cheddar cheese
1½	teaspoons paprika
1	(6-ounce) can crab meat, picked, drained

These potatoes will bring you praise every time you serve them.

▲ Preheat the oven to 400 degrees. Rub the potatoes with 1 tablespoon butter or shortening and bake for 1 hour. Increase the oven temperature to 450 degrees.

▲ Cut the potatoes into halves lengthwise and let stand until cool enough to handle. Scoop out the pulp, reserving the shells.

▲ Whip the potato pulp with ½ cup butter, cream, salt, cayenne pepper, onion, cheese and ½ teaspoon paprika in a bowl. Gently fold in the crab meat. Spoon into the reserved shells. Sprinkle with the remaining 1 teaspoon paprika.

▲ Place on a baking sheet. Bake for 15 minutes or until heated through and light brown.

One other type of edible vegetation mentioned by Lewis and Clark was a large coarse plant with ternate leaf, the leaflets of which are three-lobed, and are covered by a woody pubescence, while the flower and fruitification resemble that of parsnip. These early explorers and the Indians ate the succulent inner stem.

NATIVE FOODS USED BY THE NEZ PERCE INDIANS OF IDAHO

Christmas Potatoes

serves eight

Ingredients

8	cups sliced potatoes
2	large onions, thinly sliced
½	teaspoon salt
¼	cup butter or margarine
3	tablespoons flour
2	cups milk
¾	teaspoon salt
¼	teaspoon white pepper
½	cup chopped fresh parsley
1	(2-ounce) jar chopped pimento, drained

Dress plain potatoes for the holiday season with this recipe.

▲ Preheat the oven to 375 degrees.

▲ Combine the potatoes, onions and ½ teaspoon salt with water to cover in a large heavy saucepan. Bring to a boil and reduce the heat. Cook for 5 minutes; drain.

▲ Melt the butter in a heavy saucepan over low heat. Stir in the flour. Cook for 1 minute, stirring constantly. Add the milk gradually. Cook over low heat until thickened, stirring constantly. Add ¾ teaspoon salt, white pepper, parsley and pimento.

▲ Spoon the potato mixture into a lightly greased 8x12-inch baking dish. Spoon the sauce over the top. Bake for 40 to 45 minutes. Garnish with fresh parsley and a tomato rose.

Sage and Garlic Mashed Potatoes

serves eight

Ingredients

1	large clove of garlic, sliced
3	tablespoons olive oil
1	tablespoon minced fresh sage leaves
2	tablespoons olive oil
12	fresh whole sage leaves
	Coarse salt to taste
4	(8-ounce) russet baking potatoes
	Salt to taste
1	cup plain yogurt
1	tablespoon unsalted butter, softened
	Pepper to taste

This dish is hearty and satisfying without being heavy.

▲ Sauté the garlic in 3 tablespoons olive oil in a small saucepan until golden brown. Stir in the minced sage and remove the saucepan from the heat. Let stand for 15 minutes. Strain and reserve the oil.

▲ Heat the remaining 2 tablespoons olive oil in a small skillet over medium-high heat. Fry the sage leaves 1 at a time in the heated oil for 3 seconds or until crisp, removing to paper towels to drain. Sprinkle with coarse salt.

▲ Peel the potatoes and cut into quarters. Combine with enough salted cold water in a saucepan to cover by 1 inch. Simmer for 20 minutes or until tender. Drain, reserving ⅓ cup liquid.

▲ Preheat the oven to 350 degrees.

▲ Press the warm potatoes through a ricer or medium disk of a food mill. Combine with the yogurt, butter and reserved seasoned oil in a bowl. Beat until smooth, adding enough reserved potato liquid to make of the desired consistency. Season with salt and pepper.

▲ Spoon into a baking dish. Bake just until heated through. Top with the sage leaves.

Peregrine Potato Gratin with Thyme

serves ten

Ingredients

10	kalamata olives, cut into halves
¼	cup olive oil
2	onions, thinly sliced
2	cloves of garlic, minced
2	tablespoons olive oil
2¼	pounds white potatoes, peeled, very thinly sliced
3	tablespoons fresh thyme leaves
½	teaspoon salt
	Freshly ground pepper to taste

Serve this dish at room temperature. It can be made in advance and refrigerated. Let stand for two hours before serving and garnish with olives.

▲ Marinate the olives in ¼ cup olive oil in a bowl in the refrigerator for 8 hours. Drain, reserving the oil.

▲ Preheat the oven to 400 degrees. Oil a 2½-quart baking dish with some of the reserved olive oil.

▲ Sauté the onions and garlic in 2 tablespoons heated olive oil in a large skillet over medium-low heat for 15 minutes. Layer ⅓ of the potato slices, half the onion slices, ⅓ of the reserved oil, thyme, salt and pepper in the prepared dish. Repeat the layers, reserving some of the thyme for garnish. Add the remaining potatoes and top with the remaining oil and seasonings.

▲ Bake, covered, for 20 minutes. Bake, uncovered, for 25 minutes longer. Broil just until brown. Serve at room temperature. Top with the olives and reserved thyme.

SHAFER BUTTE BARLEY PILAF

serves eight

Ingredients

7 to 8	tablespoons butter
2	cups chopped onions
1	cup sliced mushrooms
2	cups barley
1	cup dry white wine
2	cups beef broth
1	teaspoon chervil or parsley
	Cayenne pepper to taste

▲ Preheat the oven to 350 degrees and spread a large baking dish with 2 tablespoons of the butter.

▲ Sauté the onions in the remaining butter in a large skillet over medium heat until translucent. Add the mushrooms and sauté until golden brown.

▲ Stir in the barley and cook until it begins to brown. Add the wine, broth, chervil, and cayenne. Spoon into the prepared baking dish. Bake, covered, for 50 minutes. Serve immediately.

Ladders were homemade as were his various sleds. Used not only in winter but as stoneboats or slips, these contrivances were convenient ways of transporting small loads of hay, grain, or rock from a field, or anything that had to be moved. In addition, he made knives from worn out saws and files…the kitchen table and chairs, and the cupboards with their doors, hinges, and shelves…what wagon iron he needed, he forged himself out of scrap iron…even skis were homemade.

IDAHO FOLKLIFE: HOMESTEADS TO HEADSTONES

Very good

Idaho City Fiesta Rice

serves twelve

Ingredients

2	cups uncooked white rice
1	(15-ounce) can black beans, drained, rinsed
1	(15-ounce) can yellow corn, drained, rinsed
1	large red bell pepper, chopped
1	(4-ounce) can chopped green chiles
½	cup chopped green onions
½	cup chopped fresh cilantro
½	cup chopped black olives
½	cup chopped green olives
¼	cup fresh orange juice
2	tablespoons lime juice
2	tablespoons olive oil
2	teaspoons ground cumin
½	teaspoon chili powder *more*
1	teaspoon salt

add more and/or add sherry vinegar

Makes tons

For a fat-free version of this dish, omit the olives and olive oil.

▲ Cook the rice using the package directions. Spoon into a large bowl and fluff with a fork. Cool to room temperature.

▲ Add the beans, corn, bell pepper, green chiles, green onions, cilantro and olives. Add the orange juice, lime juice, olive oil, cumin, chili powder and salt and toss lightly.

▲ Store for up to 2 days in the refrigerator. Serve chilled or at room temperature.

Lucky Peak Jasmine Rice

serves six

Ingredients

2	tablespoons oyster sauce
1	teaspoon sugar
8	ounces thickly sliced bacon
1½	tablespoons peanut oil
5	eggs, beaten
	Pepper to taste
1	tablespoon peanut oil
3	medium shallots, minced
1¼	cups chopped broccoli stems
3	cups jasmine rice cooked in chicken stock, cooled
6	medium scallions, thinly sliced
	Salt to taste

▲ Mix the oyster sauce and sugar in a bowl and set aside.

▲ Cut the fat from the bacon and cut the lean portion into ½-inch pieces. Cut the fat into pieces. Heat a wok over high heat for 40 seconds. Add the fat and stir-fry for 2 minutes or until golden brown and crisp. Remove with a slotted spoon to drain on paper towels. Rinse and dry the wok.

▲ Heat the wok over high heat for 40 seconds. Add 1½ tablespoons peanut oil and swirl in the wok with a spatula for 1 minute or until a wisp of white smoke appears. Add the eggs and pepper. Cook for 2 minutes or until firmly scrambled, stirring constantly. Remove to a plate and cut into ½-inch pieces. Rinse and dry the wok.

▲ Heat the wok over high heat for 40 seconds. Add 1 tablespoon peanut oil and heat as above. Add the lean bacon in a single layer. Cook for 1 minute. Turn and cook until browned. Stir in the shallots and cook for 2 minutes longer or until softened. Add the broccoli. Stir-fry for 2 minutes.

▲ Stir in the rice. Cook for 2 minutes or until heated through. Add the oyster sauce mixture and stir to coat the rice well. Stir in the eggs, scallions and salt. Spoon onto a warm platter and top with the crisp bacon cracklings.

Boise River Rice and Pineapple

serves ten

Ingredients

2½	cups uncooked rice
1	medium onion, chopped
2	tablespoons butter
2	(10-ounce) cans beef broth
2	(10-ounce) cans beef consommé
1	teaspoon garlic salt
2	tablespoons melted butter
2	(13-ounce) cans pineapple chunks, drained
¼	cup melted butter
1½	teaspoons curry powder

This is an ideal complement to beef or lamb and still tastes good even if you reduce the amount of butter slightly.

▲ Preheat the oven to 350 degrees and butter a 2½-quart baking dish.

▲ Brown the rice in a large skillet, stirring constantly; spoon into the prepared baking dish. Sauté the onion in 2 tablespoons butter until translucent. Add the broth, consommé, garlic salt and 2 tablespoons melted butter. Stir into the rice.

▲ Bake, covered, for 1 hour. Combine the pineapple chunks, ¼ cup butter and curry powder and stir into the rice. Bake for 20 minutes longer or until the rice is tender.

The birds in the sky and the wind in the grass told us the earth was our gift from the Father and it belongs to us all.

SHOSHONI INDIAN PROVERB

SILVER CITY WILD RICE

serves six

Ingredients

1½	cups uncooked wild rice
4	(10-ounce) cans consommé
¾	cup chopped red or green bell pepper
1	cup chopped onion
¼	cup butter
1	cup sliced mushrooms
1	cup cream
½	cup chopped walnuts (optional)
	Salt and pepper to taste

This is a delicious, no-fail recipe!

▲ Soak the wild rice in water in a bowl for 2 to 3 hours. Preheat the oven to 350 degrees and butter a baking dish.

▲ Cook the rice, covered, in the consommé in a saucepan for 1 hour or until the liquid is absorbed.

▲ Sauté the bell pepper and onion in the butter until the onion is translucent. Add the mushrooms and cook just until tender. Toss with the rice and add the cream and walnuts. Season with salt and pepper to taste. Spoon into the prepared baking dish.

▲ Bake, uncovered, for 25 minutes or until bubbly. Serve immediately.

But here in Idaho the traveler will encounter…a practical Eden at various stages of his journey. He will find here and there in the midst of these plains luxuriant crops, emerald or golden, trees blossom and perfume-laden, or bending to earth with their lavish foliage. Boise City, fairly embowered in flower gardens and fruit orchards, and thousands of acres of land…

IDAHO TERRITORY 1881

Roasted Garlic and Wild Mushroom Risotto

serves six

Ingredients

2	large heads of garlic, cloves separated, unpeeled
2	tablespoons olive oil
¾	ounce dried wild mushrooms
1	tablespoon olive oil
8	ounces mixed fresh wild stemmed shiitake or crimini mushrooms, sliced, or button mushrooms
	Salt and pepper to taste
1	cup chopped shallots
2	tablespoons chopped fresh thyme or 2 teaspoons dried thyme
1	tablespoon olive oil
1½	cups arborio rice or medium grain white rice
½	cup dry white wine
4	cups (or less) canned reduced-sodium chicken broth
2	cups thinly sliced fresh spinach leaves
½	cup freshly grated Parmesan cheese

▲ Preheat the oven to 400 degrees.

▲ Combine the garlic cloves and 2 tablespoons olive oil in a small baking dish. Bake for 50 minutes or until golden brown and tender when pierced with a sharp knife, stirring occasionally. Cool slightly. Peel the garlic and measure a packed ¼ cup. Refrigerate any remaining garlic for another use.

▲ Place the dried mushrooms in a small bowl and add enough hot water to just cover. Let stand for 30 minutes or until soft. Drain, squeeze mushrooms dry and chop coarsely.

▲ Heat 1 tablespoon oil in a large nonstick skillet over medium-high heat. Add the fresh mushrooms and sauté for 7 minutes or until golden brown and juices evaporate. Add the dried mushrooms and sauté for 1 minute. Season with salt and pepper and set aside.

▲ Sauté the shallots and thyme in 1 tablespoon heated olive oil in a heavy medium saucepan over medium-high heat for 4 minutes or until tender. Stir in the rice and wine. Cook until the liquid has nearly evaporated.

▲ Mix in the chopped garlic and 3½ cups chicken broth and bring to a boil. Reduce the heat and cook for 20 minutes or until the rice is tender and the mixture is creamy, stirring occasionally. Add more broth if risotto is dry. Add the mushroom mixture and spinach. Cook until the spinach wilts, stirring constantly. Stir in the cheese. Adjust seasonings.

ATHENIAN ORZO

serves four

Ingredients

1	small onion, chopped
4	cloves of garlic, minced
1½	teaspoons olive oil
¼	cup dry white wine
1	(28-ounce) can tomatoes, drained, chopped
3	tablespoons chopped fresh parsley
1	tablespoon capers
½	teaspoon oregano
½	teaspoon basil
	Red pepper flakes to taste
½	teaspoon salt
¼	teaspoon freshly ground pepper
1	cup uncooked orzo
	Salt to taste
½	cup crumbled feta cheese

Orzo, a rice-shaped pasta, makes a delightful base for this Greek dish. To serve as a main dish, add one pound of peeled medium shrimp and the liquid from the tomatoes.

▲ Preheat the oven to 450 degrees.

▲ Sauté the onion and garlic in the heated olive oil in a 2-quart saucepan over medium heat for 3½ minutes or until tender. Add the wine. Cook for 1 minute.

▲ Stir in the tomatoes, half the parsley, capers, oregano, basil, red pepper flakes, ½ teaspoon salt and pepper. Cook until heated through.

▲ Cook the orzo in boiling water with salt to taste in a saucepan for 10 minutes or until tender but still firm; drain. Combine with the tomato mixture.

▲ Spoon into a baking dish. Sprinkle with the cheese and the remaining parsley. Bake for 10 minutes or until the cheese is bubbly.

Pasta and Artichokes in Garlic Cream Sauce

serves eight

Ingredients

14	ounces uncooked pasta shells
1	teaspoon salt
8	cups water
3½	tablespoons butter or margarine
2	cloves of garlic, chopped
1½	tablespoons flour
1	cup half-and-half
½	cup freshly grated Parmesan cheese
½	cup chopped fresh parsley
1	(6-ounce) jar marinated artichoke hearts, drained, cut into halves
2	large nectarines, cut into wedges
	Salt and pepper to taste

▲ Cook the pasta al dente with 1 teaspoon salt in boiling water in a saucepan and drain.

▲ Melt the butter in a medium saucepan over medium heat. Add the garlic and sauté for 1 minute or just until golden brown. Remove from the heat and stir in the flour, blending until smooth.

▲ Return to the heat and stir in the half-and-half, cheese and parsley gradually. Cook until thickened and smooth, stirring constantly.

▲ Stir in the hot pasta, artichoke hearts and nectarine wedges. Cook until heated through. Season to taste.

A demure Victorian woman, Marie Irvin came overland by train from New York and was immediately captivated by the frontier atmosphere and beauty of the rising Boise foothills. She arrived in 1898, a period caught between the pioneers and a new era. Marie Irvin was well educated in Eastern art schools and painted in oils and watercolors, created prints, and designed wall coverings…

ONE HUNDRED YEARS OF IDAHO ART

Snake River Canyon Mushroom Pasta

serves four

Ingredients

8	ounces uncooked penne, orecchiette, rotelle or spaghetti
2	tablespoons olive oil
16	ounces fresh mushrooms, cut into halves
3	cloves of garlic, minced
⅔	cup white wine
2	large tomatoes, cut into ¾-inch chunks
¾	cup sliced green onions
½	cup packed chopped Italian parsley (cilantro) and/or basil leaves
	Salt and freshly ground pepper to taste

▲ Cook the pasta al dente using the package directions; drain and keep hot.

▲ Heat the olive oil in a large skillet over medium-high heat. Add the mushrooms and garlic and sauté for 4 minutes, tossing occasionally. Add the wine, bring to a boil and cook until the liquid is reduced by ½. Stir in the tomatoes, green onions, parsley and basil. Cook until just heated through.

▲ Remove from the heat and season with salt and pepper. Toss with the hot pasta in a serving bowl. Garnish servings with grated Parmesan or Romano cheese.

In the fall, if one was prudent, one killed animals and made jerky…herbs could be dried. Eventually, following the pack trains, wagon trains brought in a greater variety of foods such as rice and beans and canned foods, but if one planned to stay in the wilderness in the winter, those dried foods would have to be purchased in large quantities to last through the winter, planning also for the mice and pack rats who always managed to work their way into the supplies…

FOOTPRINTS ON MOUNTAIN TRAILS

Pasta with Spinach and Almonds

serves four

Ingredients

8	ounces uncooked penne, ziti or corkscrew pasta
2	teaspoons salt
2	tablespoons sliced almonds
1	teaspoon olive oil
1	clove of garlic, minced
1	pound spinach, coarsely chopped
3	tablespoons golden raisins
½	teaspoon instant vegetable bouillon
¾	teaspoon salt
2	medium plum tomatoes, peeled, seeded, chopped
3	tablespoons grated Parmesan cheese

This delicious new twist on pasta primavera is delicious and low in fat.

▲ Cook the pasta with 2 teaspoons salt in a saucepan using the package directions. Toast the almonds in a nonstick 12-inch skillet until golden brown, stirring and shaking frequently. Remove from the skillet.

▲ Add the olive oil and garlic to the skillet and sauté until the garlic is golden brown. Increase the heat to medium-high and add the spinach, raisins, bouillon and ¾ teaspoon salt. Cook just until the spinach wilts.

▲ Drain the pasta and return to the saucepan. Add the spinach mixture and tomatoes. Cook until heated through. Add 2 tablespoons of the Parmesan cheese and toss to mix well.

▲ Spoon into 4 serving bowls and top with the almonds and remaining 1 tablespoon Parmesan cheese.

Falcon Spinach Lasagna

serves eight

Ingredients

2	pounds fresh spinach
¼	cup vegetable oil
1	onion, chopped
3	cloves of garlic, minced
2	pounds fresh mushrooms, sliced
¼	teaspoon dried red pepper flakes
2	cups ricotta cheese
1	cup grated Parmesan cheese
3	tablespoons chopped fresh basil or 1 tablespoon dried basil
¼	teaspoon pepper
8	ounces uncooked lasagna noodles
1¼	cups shredded extra-sharp Cheddar cheese
4	cups shredded mozzarella cheese
1	(4-ounce) jar roasted sweet red peppers, drained, cut into thin strips

This dish may be covered and refrigerated for up to two days before serving. Let stand at room temperature for at least two hours. Bake, covered, at 350 degrees for 20 minutes and uncovered for 10 minutes longer.

▲ Preheat the oven to 350 degrees. Wash the spinach leaves and discard the stems. Dry and tear into 2-inch pieces.

▲ Heat the oil in a large skillet and sauté the onion and garlic until tender. Add the mushrooms and red pepper flakes and cook over medium-high heat just until the mushrooms are tender. Pile the spinach on top and stir in. Cook until the spinach is wilted.

▲ Combine the ricotta cheese, Parmesan cheese, basil and pepper in a medium bowl and mix well.

▲ Spread ⅓ of the spinach mixture in a 9x13-inch baking pan. Layer with half the lasagna noodles and then ⅓ of the spinach mixture. Cover with the entire ricotta mixture, smoothing as evenly as possible. Sprinkle with half the Cheddar cheese and half the mozzarella cheese. Add the roasted red pepper strips. Cover with the remaining lasagna noodles, overlapping them if necessary. Top with the remaining spinach mixture and any liquid remaining in the pan.

▲ Place the baking pan on a baking sheet. Bake for 15 minutes. Sprinkle with the remaining Cheddar cheese and mozzarella cheese. Bake for 15 or 20 minutes longer or until the lasagna is bubbly and the cheese is golden brown. Let stand for 15 minutes before serving.

Gallery Five

Meat and Wild Game

South Central Idaho

The falls at Shoshone are deeper than Niagara and the sand
dunes at Bruneau are the tallest in North America. It is a land
of bubbling hot mineral water, underground rivers, and ice
blue pure springs cascading out of rocky Snake River canyon walls.
Conestoga wagons crossed the Snake at Three Mile Island as
they made their lonely way West on the Oregon Trail. Echoes of
overland pioneers still linger on quiet starry nights.

Breath of the mountains
Blow down the valleys
Bring joy to the people
Who live by the river.

— Gray Elk
Native of the Shoshoni-Bannock tribe of Idaho

Bruneau Dunes Brunch

Breakfast Soufflé, page 98

Birds of Prey Fruit Compote, page 99

Long Valley Oatmeal Carrot Bread, page 81

Hill House Cinnamon Rolls, page 74

Cascade Banana Bread, page 80

Sunshine Berry Coffee Cake, page 75

Fourth of July Pass Caffé Latté Punch, page 38

Johannisberg Riesling

Special Harvest Champagne

Beef and Asparagus Rolls with Bleu Cheese Sauce

serves four

Beef

8	(2½-ounce) thin boneless beef or veal cutlets
	Salt and pepper to taste
8	asparagus spears
8	thin slices cooked ham or pro-sciutto
1	tablespoon olive oil

Bleu Cheese Sauce

2	tablespoons butter
1½	tablespoons flour
¼	cup dry white wine
1	cup milk
¼	cup shredded Cheddar cheese
¾	cup crumbled bleu cheese
	Salt and pepper to taste

▲ For the beef, preheat the broiler. Sprinkle the steaks with salt and pepper and place between sheets of waxed paper. Pound the steaks until thin and tenderized.

▲ Trim the asparagus to a uniform length and parboil in lightly salted water in a saucepan for 3 minutes. Drain and cool under cold running water. Drain again.

▲ Place a slice of ham and an asparagus spear on each steak and roll to enclose the asparagus. Secure with wooden picks and brush with the oil.

▲ Place on a rack in a broiler pan. Broil until done to taste, turning frequently.

▲ For the sauce, melt the butter in a saucepan over medium heat. Add the flour and cook for several minutes to form a roux. Whisk in the wine and milk. Cook until thickened, stirring constantly. Reduce the heat and add the cheeses. Continue stirring until the cheeses are melted and the sauce is creamy. Season with salt and pepper.

▲ Arrange the beef rolls on a platter and top with the sauce. Serve immediately.

Beef with Broccoli in Oyster Sauce

serves four

Beef Marinade

1	tablespoon light soy sauce
1	tablespoon Chinese cooking wine or dry sherry
2	teaspoons cornstarch
½	teaspoon sugar
1	teaspoon sesame oil
½	teaspoon baking soda or ½ peeled and grated kiwi

Beef

1	(1- to 1¼-pound) flank steak, thinly sliced
1	tablespoon vegetable oil
1¼	pounds (about) fresh broccoli florets
¼	cup vegetable oil
2	cloves of garlic, finely chopped
4	scallions, white parts only, cut into ½-inch pieces
4	slices fresh ginger, cut into strips
2	tablespoons oyster sauce
1	teaspoon vinegar
1	tablespoon cornstarch
½	cup beef stock
1	red bell pepper, thinly sliced

▲ For the marinade, combine the soy sauce, wine, cornstarch, sugar, sesame oil, and baking soda in a bowl.

▲ For the beef, pour the marinade over the slices of steak and marinate for 20 minutes; drain. Add 1 tablespoon oil to the beef to keep the slices separated.

▲ Steam the broccoli over boiling water for 4 minutes. Drain and place around the edges of a platter.

▲ Heat a wok or large skillet over medium-high heat and add ¼ cup oil. Sauté the garlic for 1 minute. Add the beef and stir-fry until cooked through. Add the scallions and ginger. Stir-fry for several minutes. Add the oyster sauce and vinegar, tossing lightly.

▲ Combine the cornstarch and broth and stir into the beef mixture. Cook until thickened, stirring constantly. Spoon into the center of the platter and top with the red pepper strips. Serve immediately with rice.

Bruneau Dunes Stuffed Flank Steak

serves eight

Ingredients

1½	cups freshly grated Parmesan or Romano cheese
½	cup soft bread crumbs
2	(6-ounce) jars marinated artichoke hearts, drained, chopped
2	cups finely chopped green onions
1	pound bacon, chopped, crisp-fried, drained
2	cups chopped fresh spinach
1	cup minced fresh parsley
½	cup chopped mushrooms
2	(1½-pound) beef flank steaks, tenderized
	Worcestershire sauce to taste
2 to 4	cloves of garlic, minced
2	tablespoons butter
2½	cups strong beef broth
8	ounces mushrooms, sliced
1	large onion, thinly sliced
	Several sprigs of fresh parsley

If your personal taste or diet doesn't allow artichoke hearts, bacon or mushrooms, simply omit them from the recipe.

▲ Preheat the oven to 300 degrees.

▲ Mix the Parmesan cheese, bread crumbs, artichoke hearts, green onions, bacon, spinach, ½ cup of the parsley and ½ cup mushrooms in a large bowl. Pat half of the mixture evenly onto each of the flank steaks. Roll the steaks carefully to enclose the filling and tie in 6 or 8 places with cotton twine, sealing the ends well.

▲ Rub the steaks with Worcestershire sauce and minced garlic. Sear on all sides in the butter in a heated skillet until brown. Place in a roasting pan.

▲ Remove the skillet from heat. Pour the broth into the skillet, stirring to deglaze. Add 8 ounces mushrooms, onion and the remaining ½ cup parsley and pour over the meat rolls.

▲ Roast, covered, for 45 to 60 minutes or until fork tender. Remove the rolls from the pan and let rest for 5 to 10 minutes before slicing. Arrange on a platter in a pinwheel fashion and garnish with the parsley sprigs. Serve with the mushroom sauce.

Meat

Moonstone Mountain Flank Steak with Brandy Sauce

serves three

Ingredients

2	tablespoons butter, softened
2	tablespoons Dijon mustard
1½	teaspoons Worcestershire sauce
¾	teaspoon curry powder
¼	teaspoon crushed mustard seeds
1	clove of garlic, crushed
	Salt and pepper to taste
1	(1- to 2-pound) flank steak
¼	cup sherry or Madeira
¼	cup white wine vinegar
2	tablespoons butter
8	ounces fresh mushrooms, sliced
1	shallot, minced
¾	cup sour cream
3	tablespoons brandy

▲ Combine 2 tablespoons butter, mustard, Worcestershire sauce, curry powder, mustard seeds, garlic, salt and pepper in a bowl and mix into a paste. Spread over the flank steak and place in a shallow glass dish.

▲ Pour the wine and vinegar over the steak and cover loosely. Marinate in the refrigerator for 8 hours. Let stand at room temperature for 2 hours.

▲ Preheat the broiler and place the steak on the rack in a broiler pan.

▲ Broil for 2 to 3 minutes on each side for rare or to taste. Remove the steak to a heated platter and cover loosely to keep warm.

▲ Melt 2 tablespoons butter in a skillet and add the mushrooms and shallot. Sauté over medium heat until tender. Remove from the heat and set aside.

▲ Place the broiler pan with meat juices on the stove top over medium-high heat. Stir in the sour cream and brandy gradually. Simmer for 4 minutes, stirring constantly. Blend in the mushroom and shallot mixture and cook until heated through. Serve with the steak.

Rattlesnake Creek Peppercorn Roast Beef

serves ten

Roast Marinade

1	tablespoon tomato paste
½	teaspoon garlic powder
1	cup soy sauce
¾	cup vinegar

Beef

1	(5- to 6-pound) boneless rib eye roast
½	cup coarsely ground green or black peppercorns
½	teaspoon ground cardamom seeds
1½	tablespoons cornstarch
¼	cup cold water

You may serve the roast au jus if you prefer, rather than thickening the cooking juices for gravy.

▲ For the marinade, combine the tomato paste, garlic powder, soy sauce and vinegar in a bowl and mix well.

▲ For the beef, rub the roast with the peppercorns and cardamom. Combine with the marinade in a bowl. Marinate in the refrigerator for 24 hours.

▲ Preheat the oven to 300 degrees.

▲ Bring the roast to room temperature and remove from the marinade. Wrap in foil and place in a shallow roasting pan. Roast for 2 hours for medium-rare. Drain and reserve the drippings.

▲ Increase the oven temperature to 350 degrees and brown the uncovered roast. Remove from the oven and let rest for 10 minutes before serving.

▲ Strain the pan drippings into a saucepan, skimming off the fat. Add 1 cup of water for each cup of meat juices. Bring to a boil and add marinade to taste for flavor. Dissolve the cornstarch in the cold water. Stir into the drippings and cook until thickened, stirring constantly. Serve with the roast.

Grilled Asian Prime Rib Rolls
serves three

Ingredients

12	(5- to 6-inch) fresh asparagus spears
12	(½ x 5- to 6-inch) carrot strips
1	pound boneless prime rib
2 to 3	tablespoons cornstarch
2	tablespoons sugar
6	tablespoons water
3	tablespoons sake
3	tablespoons mirin
¼	cup soy sauce

The mirin in this recipe is a low-alcohol Japanese sweet rice wine available in Asian markets and many supermarkets. This marinade tenderizes the beef so that the rolls will grill very quickly.

▲ Steam the asparagus and carrot strips until tender-crisp.

▲ Slice the beef into 12 thin 4x6-inch pieces. Arrange each two slices to overlap slightly, forming a 6x6-inch square. Brush lightly with the cornstarch and place 2 asparagus spears and 2 carrot sticks across the seam. Roll the beef to enclose the vegetables and secure with cotton twine. Place in a nonreactive bowl.

▲ Combine the sugar, water, sake, mirin and soy sauce and pour over beef rolls. Marinate in the refrigerator for several hours.

▲ Preheat the grill. Soak bamboo skewers in water for 30 minutes. Put a skewer into each end of the beef rolls. Grill the rolls quickly on both sides.

▲ Heat the marinade in a saucepan. Remove the skewers and twine and slice the rolls into 1½-inch pieces. Stand the slices on warmed serving plates so that the vegetables are visible. Spoon the heated marinade around the rolls.

Meat

Mountain Home Marinated Steak
serves four

Ingredients

¼   cup soy sauce
3   tablespoons honey
2   tablespoons vinegar
1½ teaspoons garlic powder
1½ teaspoons ginger
¾   cup vegetable oil
1   green onion, finely chopped
1   tablespoon lime juice
1   (1½-pound) flank or top sir-
    loin steak

▲ Combine the soy sauce, honey and vinegar in a bowl. Stir in the garlic powder, ginger, oil, green onion and lime juice. Pour over the steak in a shallow dish. Marinate in the refrigerator for 4 hours or longer.

▲ Bring the steak to room temperature and preheat the broiler or grill. Remove the steak from the dish and reserve the marinade.

▲ Cook for 3 to 5 minutes on each side or until done to taste, basting occasionally with the marinade.

▲ Let rest for 5 minutes and then slice diagonally before serving.

"My days were full…as they started at 6 o'clock when I went over to a nearby barn; fed, watered and milked the cow; returning to the house to strain the milk, put it away and start the fire. Then I got the children up to dress while I went to the schoolhouse to build a fire and return to prepare breakfast. After feeding the chickens, I went back to the school…after a day of classes, I swept the school floors with an oil and sawdust mixture, and with my son's help, carried in large chunks of wood for the next day's fire."

SALMON RIVER SAGA

Shoshone Sirloin in Red Wine Sauce

serves eight

Ingredients

1	cup finely chopped green onions including tops
2	tablespoons finely chopped shallots (optional)
½	bay leaf, crumbled
1	teaspoon minced fresh thyme or ½ teaspoon dried
2	tablespoons butter
1½	cups dry red wine
1	(3½-pound) boneless beef sirloin steak, about 1½ inches thick
2	tablespoons butter
3	tablespoons minced fresh parsley
1	tablespoon fresh lemon juice
1	tablespoon flour

▲ Sauté the green onions, shallots, bay leaf and thyme in 2 tablespoons butter in a heavy skillet over medium-high heat for 2 to 3 minutes or until tender. Add the wine and cook until reduced by ⅓. Pour into a bowl and reserve.

▲ Sear the steak in the same skillet over high heat for 1½ minutes on each side. Reduce the heat to medium and let the skillet cool slightly. Return the sauce to the skillet and add the remaining 2 tablespoons butter, parsley, lemon juice and flour. Cook the steak for an additional 2 to 4 minutes on each side or until done to taste.

▲ Remove the steak to a serving platter and let rest for 5 minutes before slicing into 2-inch diagonal strips. Serve with the red wine sauce.

When professional artists like Thomas Moran and James Everett Stuart came west before the turn of the century, their route through the region usually included a stop at Shoshone Falls, one of southern Idaho's most remarkable landmarks. Some artists felt that Shoshone Falls, which was forty-five feet higher than Niagara Falls, rivaled its Eastern rival in both splendor and grandeur…

ONE HUNDRED YEARS OF IDAHO ART

Meat

Beef Stew with Red Wine and Polenta

serves six

Beef Stew

4	pounds beef chuck
3	tablespoons extra-virgin olive oil
1	large onion, minced
¼	cup chopped Italian parsley
3	cloves of garlic, chopped
2	bay leaves
¼	teaspoon cloves
¼	teaspoon cinnamon
¼	teaspoon allspice
1	cup dry red wine
2¼	cups beef stock or broth
2	(14-ounce) cans Italian plum tomatoes
½	cup pitted Niçoise olives
4	teaspoons chopped fresh rosemary or 2 teaspoons dried rosemary
2	red bell peppers, cut into ¼ inch strips
	Salt and pepper to taste

Polenta

1½	teaspoons salt
9	cups water
2	cups cornmeal

▲ Cut the beef into 1-inch cubes. Brown in batches in the heated olive oil in a Dutch oven over high heat, removing the beef as it browns.

▲ Add the onion and parsley to the Dutch oven. Cook until the onion is golden brown. Add the garlic, bay leaves, cloves, cinnamon, allspice and beef.

▲ Stir in the red wine and simmer for 10 minutes. Add the beef stock and simmer for 10 minutes. Add the undrained tomatoes, breaking up the tomatoes with a spoon. Stir in the olives and rosemary. Simmer, covered, for 1½ hours.

▲ Add the bell peppers. Cook for 15 minutes longer. Season with salt and pepper. Discard the bay leaves.

▲ For the polenta, bring the salted water to a boil in a large heavy saucepan. Whisk in the cornmeal gradually. Cook until the mixture boils and thickens, whisking constantly. Reduce the heat and simmer for 30 minutes or until done to taste.

▲ Spoon the polenta into shallow bowls. Spoon the stew over the polenta.

Meat

Curried Beef and Pasta in Tomato Sauce
serves six

Ingredients

½	cup butter
3½	cups tomato purée
3½	cups canned whole tomatoes
1	large yellow onion, sliced
2	dried whole hot red peppers
1	clove of garlic
2½	tablespoons curry powder
1	tablespoon turmeric
2	tablespoons peanut oil
1	pound lean beef, ground or cubed
12	ounces spinach pasta, cooked al dente

▲ Melt the butter in a deep heavy saucepan over medium heat. Add the tomato purée, tomatoes, onion, red peppers, garlic, curry powder and turmeric. Simmer for 1 hour, stirring occasionally. Remove the hot peppers.

▲ Heat the oil in a large heavy skillet over medium-high heat. Add the beef and sauté until cooked through. Add to the tomato sauce.

▲ Toss with the hot pasta in a serving bowl and serve immediately.

In 1895, there were no homesteads on the River. A few aging miners lived in hillside dugouts, the nearest approach to houses. Food staples were flour, beans, lard, salt, coffee and sugar. Saddle horses were grazed out in the open…there were no fences. No one, up to that time, had come expecting to stay.

SALMON RIVER SAGA

Oregon Trail Barbecued Lamb

serves eight

Ingredients

1	teaspoon rosemary
1	teaspoon thyme
1	teaspoon marjoram
1	teaspoon salt
½	teaspoon oregano
½	cup olive oil
2	tablespoons chopped green onions
¼	teaspoon pepper
½	teaspoon Worcestershire sauce
1	cup dry red wine
2	cloves of garlic, minced
1	(6-pound) leg of lamb, boned, butterflied

▲ Combine the rosemary, thyme, marjoram, salt, oregano, oil, green onions, pepper, Worcestershire sauce, wine and garlic. Pour over the leg of lamb in a dish. Marinate in the refrigerator for 24 hours, turning frequently.

▲ Return the lamb to room temperature and preheat the grill.

▲ Grill the lamb over medium coals for 45 minutes or until done to taste. Let rest for 10 minutes before slicing.

The dictates of topography primarily determined where the influx of population came into the Northwest territories. The easiest corridors through mountain passes became the principal routes. A number of early immigrants came by way of a South Pass route into Idaho from Wyoming, ultimately traveling on to Oregon or California. The trickle became a flood and the trail west along the Snake River through Idaho became a clearly defined portion of the Oregon Trail...

ONE HUNDRED YEARS OF IDAHO ART

Butterflied Idaho Spring Lamb with Lemon Mustard Sauce

serves ten

Ingredients

1	(7- to 8-pound) leg of lamb, boned, butterflied
	Salt and pepper to taste
2	large cloves of garlic, minced
6	tablespoons unsalted butter
3	tablespoons coarse-grain mustard
	Grated rind of 2 lemons
	Juice of 1 lemon
¼	teaspoon oregano

▲ Preheat the broiler and place the oven rack 6 inches from the heat source.

▲ Place the leg of lamb fat side up in a shallow pan. Broil for 10 to 15 minutes. Turn and broil for 8 to 10 minutes longer or to 135 degrees on a meat thermometer. Remove to a serving platter and season with salt and pepper. Let stand for 10 to 15 minutes.

▲ Sauté the garlic in the butter in a small saucepan over low heat for 3 to 5 minutes. Whisk in the mustard, lemon rind, lemon juice and oregano and cook for several minutes. Carve the lamb and serve with the sauce.

Thousand Springs Stir-Fried Lamb with Garlic

serves four

Ingredients

12	ounces boneless lean lamb
2	teaspoons rice wine or dry sherry
2	teaspoons each dark soy sauce and light soy sauce
½	teaspoon sesame oil
2	teaspoons vegetable oil
1½	teaspoons minced scallions
3	cloves of garlic, sliced
½	teaspoon minced gingerroot

This is delicious served with rice and stir-fried broccoli.

▲ Cut the lamb into thin slices and combine with the rice wine, soy sauces and sesame oil in a bowl; mix well. Marinate for 20 minutes; drain most of the marinade.

▲ Heat a wok or large skillet and add the vegetable oil. Add the lamb and stir-fry for 2 minutes. Add the scallions, garlic and ginger. Stir-fry for 4 minutes longer.

In Idaho, George Catlin and Gustavius Sohon were among the first artists to portray native Americans in their homeland, while James Wilkins was one of the earliest to visually record the actual wagon migration west. Although most artists of this period worked on relatively small paper, necessitated by the inconvenience of travel, they presented their subjects in a grand-scale fashion. Landscapes...emphasize great distance and spacious skies.

ONE HUNDRED YEARS OF IDAHO ART

Rack of Lamb in a Pecan Crust

serves four

Lamb

¼	cup unsalted butter
1	clove of garlic, minced
2	teaspoons minced rosemary
½	cup coarsely ground toasted bread crumbs
½	cup ground toasted pecans
	Salt and pepper to taste
2	(2½-pound) trimmed racks of lamb or loin chops

Wine Sauce

6	tablespoons unsalted butter
½	cup mushrooms with stems
1	carrot, peeled and chopped
1	stalk celery, chopped
½	small onion, chopped
1	teaspoon minced shallot
1	teaspoon minced garlic
½	cup chopped fresh parsley
2	teaspoons chopped rosemary
2	teaspoons chopped tarragon
2	bay leaves, crushed
2	cups Cabernet Sauvignon
2	tablespoons tomato paste
1	tomato, crushed
4	cups lamb stock or beef broth
2	tablespoons flour
1 to 2	tablespoons barbecue sauce
	Salt and pepper to taste
½	teaspoon sugar

This recipe is from The Inn at Little Washington, where it is served with shoestring sweet potatoes for a special touch. Use fresh rosemary and tarragon when available.

▲ For the lamb, melt the butter in a large skillet over medium heat. Add the garlic and rosemary and sauté for 1 minute. Stir in the bread crumbs and pecans. Cook for 5 minutes or until lightly browned and crunchy, stirring constantly. Season to taste with salt and pepper. Cover and set aside.

▲ Preheat the grill to hot and the oven to 400 degrees. Divide each rack of lamb into halves crosswise. Grill the lamb for 8 minutes or until seared on all sides. Remove to a baking dish and bake for 12 minutes or until done to taste. Remove from the oven and let rest for 10 to 20 minutes.

▲ For the sauce, melt 4 tablespoons of the butter in a large saucepan over medium heat and add the mushrooms, carrot, celery, onion, shallot, garlic, parsley, rosemary, tarragon and bay leaves. Sauté for 2 minutes and add the wine, tomato paste, tomato and stock. Boil the mixture for 20 minutes or until reduced by ½.

▲ Make a browned roux by combining the remaining 2 tablespoons butter with the flour in a small pan over medium heat. Cook until the flour begins to brown, stirring constantly. Stir the roux and 1 tablespoon barbecue sauce into the wine sauce. Simmer for 15 minutes and then strain through a fine sieve, discarding the solids. Taste the sauce and season with salt, pepper, sugar and more barbecue sauce if needed.

▲ Spread the pecan mixture on a platter. Brush the lamb with some of the sauce and roll each half rack in the mixture to form a crust. Slice the racks into chops and divide them among 4 individual plates. Spoon the sauce over the chops and serve immediately.

Lamb Skewers with Balsamic Vinegar

serves six

Ingredients

2	pounds boneless leg of lamb, cut from the sirloin
1	cup sweet marsala, preferably Florio
¼	cup white wine vinegar
	Salt and freshly ground pepper to taste
1	tablespoon dried rosemary or several sprigs of fresh rosemary
2	cloves of garlic, crushed
8	ounces pancetta, sliced
2 to 3	tablespoons balsamic vinegar

This is delicious with saffron risotta, buttered rice or roasted potatoes.

▲ Trim the fat from the lamb and cut into 2-inch cubes. Combine the marsala, white wine vinegar, salt, pepper, rosemary and garlic in a large bowl. Add the lamb and coat well. Marinate, covered, in the refrigerator for several hours. Remove the lamb to a platter with a slotted spoon and pat dry with paper towels.

▲ Preheat the grill or broiler. Thread the lamb and pancetta alternately onto skewers. Grill for 2 or 3 minutes on each side or until golden brown on the outside and pink and juicy on the inside. Brush with the balsamic vinegar.

The sun lies flat through the aspens, throwing shadows
that fall blue and twisted on the dazzling snow…

the creek rushes by, splashing over rocks.
It throws water on ice sheets that hang from fallen trees.

I want to live in this world forever.
I want it to stay rugged and hard to get into.

> *Harald Wyndham*
> *Deer Hunting in St. Charles Canyon*
> EIGHT IDAHO POETS: AN ANTHOLOGY

Very good sauce

Pork Chop Apple Bake

serves six

Ingredients

6	large (1-inch) pork chops
2	tablespoons butter
2	tablespoons steak sauce
6	cups sliced firm cooking apples
½	teaspoon grated lemon rind
1½	tablespoons lemon juice
¼	teaspoon nutmeg
½	teaspoon cinnamon
¾	cup packed brown sugar
2	tablespoons butter
¼	cup hot water

added Calvados

▲ Preheat the oven to 350 degrees.

– watch not to dry it

▲ Brown the pork chops in 2 tablespoons butter in a heavy skillet. Arrange the chops in a baking dish and sprinkle with the steak sauce.

▲ Mix together the apples, lemon rind, lemon juice, nutmeg, cinnamon and brown sugar in a bowl. Spoon over the chops and dot with 2 tablespoons butter. Add the hot water.

▲ Bake, covered, for 30 minutes. Uncover and bake for 30 minutes longer or until cooked through.

We had the advantage of organically grown foods without knowing it. Mama made huge crocks of cooked pork covered with a thick layer of lard. I remember carrot pies; they tasted just like pumpkin, only we didn't have pumpkin in those days.

Cosho Family Papers:
IDAHO WOMEN IN HISTORY

Braised Pork Loin with Red Onion, Cranberries and Cider

serves two

Ingredients

4	slices (¾-inch) pork loin or pork chops
1¼	teaspoons thyme
	Salt and pepper to taste
3	tablespoons flour
2	teaspoons butter
2	teaspoons vegetable oil
1	tablespoon butter
1	large red onion, cut into halves and sliced lengthwise
1	cup apple juice
1⅓	cups cranberries
½	cup chicken stock

▲ Pat the pork loin dry with a paper towel. Rub with the thyme, salt and pepper.

▲ Coat with the flour. Melt 2 teaspoons butter with the oil in a heavy skillet over medium-high heat. Brown the pork for about 2 minutes on each side and set aside. Wipe the skillet clean with paper towels.

▲ Add 1 tablespoon butter to the skillet and sauté the onion until golden brown. Add the apple juice and bring to a boil. Add the cranberries and stock and return to a boil.

▲ Reduce the heat and return the pork chops to the skillet. Simmer until the pork is cooked through. Remove the pork chops to heated plates.

▲ Increase the heat under the skillet and boil the sauce for two minutes or until thick enough to coat a spoon. Pour over the pork chops.

Biddy Dunn of the Custer, Idaho, Nevada House Hotel, charged a dollar for a room and 50 cents for dinner. Her menu included home grown fresh vegetables, pork and chicken, and fresh-caught fish. Every day, Biddy bought all the fish the children of Custer could catch for 25 cents a pound.

Land of the Yankee Fork:
IDAHO WOMEN IN HISTORY

Hot Springs Marinated Pork

serves eight

Ingredients

½   cup dry white wine

¼   cup vegetable oil

6   tablespoons Dijon mustard

¼   cup chopped mushrooms

2   tablespoons soy sauce

2   tablespoons fresh lemon juice

2   tablespoons minced onion

2   tablespoons butter

½   teaspoon celery seeds

½   teaspoon salt

½   teaspoon freshly ground pepper

1   (5-pound) pork loin roast, boned, tied

▲ Combine the wine, oil, mustard, mushrooms, soy sauce, lemon juice, onion, celery seeds, salt and pepper in a large bowl. Add the pork. Marinate, covered, in the refrigerator for 24 hours, turning occasionally.

▲ Preheat the oven to 350 degrees. Drain the pork, reserving the marinade. Place the pork in a baking pan.

▲ Roast for 2½ hours or to 155 to 160 degrees on a meat thermometer, basting frequently with the marinade during the last 30 minutes of roasting time.

Pork Chops with Peppery Maple Bourbon Sauce

serves four

Ingredients

4   large (1½-inch) center-cut
     pork chops
     Salt to taste
⅓   cup flour
2   tablespoons vegetable oil
¾   cup chicken stock
6   tablespoons bourbon
4½   tablespoons maple syrup
1   cup cream
     Freshly ground pepper to taste

▲ Season the pork chops with salt and coat with the flour. Brown in the heated oil in a heavy skillet for 2 minutes on each side. Remove from the skillet and set aside. Discard the oil.

▲ Add the stock, bourbon and maple syrup to the skillet. Bring to a boil, stirring to deglaze the skillet.

▲ Reduce the heat and return the chops to the skillet. Simmer until cooked through. Remove the chops to a platter.

▲ Increase the heat and boil the stock mixture until it begins to thicken. Add the cream and cook to the consistency of gravy, stirring frequently. Season with salt and pepper. Serve over the chops.

…the following provisions were listed for a transcontinental wagon journey for four persons: 824 pounds of flour, 725 of bacon, 75 of coffee, 160 of sugar, 200 of lard and suet, 200 of beans, 135 of dried peaches and apples, and 25 of salt, pepper and saleratus (baking soda). It is also suggested to include four pounds of tea…

Advice to Emigrants
BACON, BEANS AND GALLANTINES

Crown Roast of Pork with Mushroom Stuffing

serves twelve

Mushroom Stuffing

½	cup minced onion
⅔	cup butter
8	cups croutons
1	cup chopped celery
1	teaspoon salt
½	teaspoon pepper
1	teaspoon crushed thyme, marjoram or sage
1	teaspoon poultry seasoning
1	(6-ounce) can sliced mushrooms, drained, or 1 pound fresh mushrooms, sliced

Pork

1	(7½- to 8-pound) crown roast of pork, about 20 ribs
2	teaspoons salt
1	teaspoon pepper

▲ For the stuffing, sauté the onion in the butter in a large skillet until tender. Stir in some of the croutons. Sauté over low heat until golden brown, stirring constantly. Combine with the remaining croutons, celery, salt, pepper, thyme, poultry seasoning and mushrooms in a large bowl, tossing lightly.

▲ For the pork, preheat the oven to 325 degrees.

▲ Sprinkle the roast with salt and pepper and place bone ends up in a roasting pan. Wrap the bone ends with foil to prevent excessive browning. Place a small ovenproof bowl in the center of the roast to help retain its shape. Insert a meat thermometer into the thickest part of the roast.

▲ Roast for 2 to 3 hours. Replace the small bowl with the mushroom stuffing and cover just the stuffing with foil. Roast for 30 minutes. Roast, uncovered, for 30 minutes longer or to 185 degrees on the meat thermometer.

▲ Remove to a serving platter and replace the foil on the bone ends with paper frills. Slice between the ribs to serve.

Meat

Pork and Red Peppers
serves four

Ingredients

2	tablespoons minced garlic
½	teaspoon salt
1	teaspoon pepper
1	(2-pound) boneless pork tenderloin, cut into ¼-inch slices
¼	cup vegetable oil
4	medium red bell peppers, sliced
1	cup dry white wine
½	cup chicken broth
1	lemon, cut into wedges

▲ Combine the garlic, salt and pepper and spread on the pork slices. Let stand, covered, at room temperature for 2 hours or in the refrigerator for 6 hours.

▲ Brown the pork in batches in the oil in a heavy skillet. Remove from the skillet and set aside.

▲ Sauté the bell peppers in the drippings in the skillet; remove from the skillet and set aside. Add the wine and broth, stirring to deglaze. Return the pork to the skillet and simmer over low heat for 20 minutes or until tender. Return the peppers to the skillet and simmer for 5 minutes or until heated through. Remove the pork and peppers to a platter.

▲ Increase the heat under the skillet and boil the juices until reduced and slightly thickened. Pour over the pork and peppers and serve with the lemon wedges. Serve immediately.

City of Rocks Baby Back Ribs

serves two

Ingredients

1	pound baby back ribs
6 to 8	green onions
1	tablespoon dry sherry
2	tablespoons rice vinegar
3	tablespoons sugar
¼	cup soy sauce
5	tablespoons water

This recipe can be made two to three days in advance. Just reheat or finish cooking the ribs in the sauce before serving.

▲ Trim any excess fat from the ribs and cut into sections of 2 or 3 ribs each. Layer the green onions and ribs in a large Dutch oven.

▲ Combine the sherry, vinegar, sugar, soy sauce and water in a bowl and pour over ribs. Cover and bring to a boil. Reduce the heat and simmer for 2 hours or until most of the liquid has evaporated, carefully rotating the pieces and basting frequently with the sauce.

▲ Remove the ribs from the sauce near the end of the cooking process. Let the sauce cool slightly and skim the surface. Return the ribs to the pan and finish cooking. Serve immediately.

It was not until forts were constructed, military personnel were installed to protect travelers, and ferry crossings and way stations were in place, that a few settlers began to stay. Until that time, artistic images of Idaho consisted of impressions recorded by pathfinders documenting the overland experience.

ONE HUNDRED YEARS OF IDAHO ART

Garlic Pork Chops with Balsamic Vinegar

serves six

Ingredients

6	center-cut loin pork chops, about 2 pounds, trimmed
	Freshly ground pepper to taste
	Cloves of 1 head of garlic
¼	cup sweet vermouth
1	tablespoon Dijon mustard
12	ounces uncooked eggless noodles
⅓	cup balsamic vinegar
	Salt to taste

The rich taste of balsamic vinegar combines with the sweet taste of garlic in a unique sauce for this pork chop dish.

▲ Sprinkle the pork chops with pepper. Spray a large skillet with cooking spray and heat over medium-high heat. Add the pork chops.

▲ Cook for 4 to 5 minutes or until brown; turn the chops. Arrange the garlic around the chops and cook for 4 to 5 minutes longer or until brown.

▲ Mix the wine and mustard in a small bowl. Pour over the pork chops. Simmer, covered for 5 minutes or until cooked through.

▲ Cook the noodles in boiling water in a saucepan for 10 to 12 minutes or just until tender; drain. Place in a deep platter and arrange the pork chops over the top; keep warm.

▲ Add the vinegar to the sauce remaining in the skillet, stirring to deglaze. Bring to a boil and boil for 2 to 3 minutes or until reduced to about ½ cup. Season with salt. Spoon over the pork chops.

The saloon was in some respects the local art gallery. Masculine taste in paintings were hung to appeal to the local cowboys and homesteaders and often featured images of discreetly positioned voluptuous sirens in various states of undress. Women in these portraits seldom engage the viewer with a direct gaze, but appear detached as if in a dream.

ONE HUNDRED YEARS OF IDAHO ART

Pork Tenderloin à la Crème

serves four

Ingredients

8	slices bacon
8	(2-inch) slices pork tenderloin, butterflied
¼	cup brandy or cognac
2	teaspoons dry mustard
	Salt and pepper to taste
¼	cup dry white wine
2 to 3	tablespoons instant beef bouillon
2	cups heavy cream
2 to 3	tablespoons flour
4	ounces mushrooms, sliced

▲ Preheat the oven to 350 degrees.

▲ Cook the bacon partially in a skillet. Wrap one slice around the outer edge of each piece of tenderloin, securing with a wooden pick. Place in an ungreased baking dish. Drizzle with the brandy. Sprinkle with the mustard, salt and pepper.

▲ Bake for 20 to 30 minutes. Remove to a platter, cover loosely with foil and set aside.

▲ Skim the grease from the drippings and discard. Combine with the wine and bouillon in a skillet. Cook over medium heat, stirring to deglaze the skillet.

▲ Whisk the cream and flour in a bowl until smooth and then stir into the drippings. Bring to a boil and cook for 4 minutes or until thickened and smooth, stirring constantly.

▲ Add the pork to the skillet, turning to coat both sides with the cream sauce. Sprinkle the mushrooms on top. Bake, uncovered, for a few minutes or until the sauce is thickened.

Meat

Pork Tenderloin with Bacon and Onion Sauce

serves four

Onion Sauce

2	cups chopped onions
6	tablespoons butter
½	cup finely chopped mushrooms
¼	cup cornstarch
2	cups (about) chicken broth
1	cup sliced mushrooms
3½	tablespoons (or more) lemon juice
6	tablespoons white wine
	Seasoning salt to taste
	Cayenne pepper and salt to taste

Pork

4	(8-ounce) pieces well-trimmed pork tenderloin, at room temperature
	Salt and pepper to taste
8	ounces bacon, at room temperature
	Paprika to taste

▲ For the sauce, sauté the onions in the butter in a deep saucepan over medium heat until tender. Add the chopped mushrooms, sprinkle with cornstarch and stir to mix well. Cook over low heat for several minutes, stirring occasionally.

▲ Add the chicken broth and sliced mushrooms. Cook over low heat until thickened, stirring constantly. Add the lemon juice, wine, Maggi, cayenne and salt. Simmer for 2 minutes, adding additional broth if needed for the desired consistency.

▲ For the pork, preheat the broiler.

▲ Place a metal skewer through each piece of tenderloin. Season with salt and pepper and wrap with bacon, covering completely and securing with wooden picks. Place in a broiler pan.

▲ Broil for 8 to 10 minutes on each side. Remove to a serving platter and spoon the sauce over the top. Sprinkle with paprika and serve immediately.

Sausage and Wild Mushroom Lasagna

serves eight

Ingredients

2 cups shredded mozzarella cheese

2 cups grated Parmesan cheese

 Red Pepper Sauce (page 145)

3 pan-size sheets of pasta or 1 pound lasagna noodles

 Wild Mushroom Sauce (page 145)

An elegant party dish. This is well worth the time and effort required to assemble it. It can be made ahead, refrigerated or frozen and baked before serving. If frozen, thaw first, then bake.

▲ Preheat the oven to 375 degrees and oil a 9x13-inch baking dish. Toss the cheeses together in a bowl.

▲ Coat the bottom of the dish with some of the pepper sauce. Layer a sheet of pasta or 3 lasagna noodles, then ⅓ of the mushroom sauce, ⅓ of the cheese and ⅓ of the remaining pepper sauce in the prepared pan. Repeat twice, reversing the pepper sauce and cheese at the end so that the cheese is the top layer.

▲ Bake, uncovered, for 35 to 40 minutes or until bubbly, covering loosely with foil during the last 10 to 15 minutes if needed to prevent overbrowning. Let stand for 10 minutes before serving.

Meat

Lasagna Sauces

serves eight

Red Pepper Sauce

1	pound Italian sausage, casings removed
2	tablespoons olive oil
1	pound mushrooms, sliced
	Salt and black pepper to taste
2	cups chopped onions
3	large cloves of garlic, minced
¾	teaspoon rosemary
	Hot red pepper flakes to taste
4	red bell peppers, sliced
2	pounds plum tomatoes, chopped
2	tablespoons balsamic vinegar

Wild Mushroom Sauce

1½	ounces dried porcini mushrooms
1½	cups hot water
¼	cup unsalted butter
¼	cup flour
2½	cups milk
¼	teaspoon nutmeg
	Salt and pepper to taste

▲ For the red pepper sauce, brown the sausage in a heavy skillet, stirring until crumbly. Remove to a bowl with a slotted spoon. Drain, reserving 1 tablespoon of the pan drippings.

▲ Add 1 tablespoon of the oil, mushrooms, salt and pepper to the reserved pan drippings. Cook over medium heat until the liquid has evaporated. Add to the sausage.

▲ Add the remaining 1 tablespoon oil to the skillet and sauté the onions, garlic, rosemary, crushed red pepper, salt and black pepper. Stir in the bell peppers and tomatoes and cook, covered, for 20 minutes or until tender.

▲ Purée the tomato mixture in several batches in a food processor or blender and pour into a large saucepan. Stir the vinegar into the saucepan and add the sausage mixture. Simmer, uncovered, for 5 minutes.

▲ For the mushroom sauce, soak the porcini mushrooms in hot water for 30 minutes. Drain through a sieve lined with a rinsed and squeezed paper towel into a measuring cup. Reserve ½ cup of the soaking liquid. Chop the mushrooms fine.

▲ Melt the butter in a saucepan. Add the flour and cook for 3 minutes over medium heat to form a roux, stirring constantly. Whisk in the milk and the reserved soaking liquid in a stream and bring to a boil. Stir in the mushrooms, nutmeg, salt and pepper and simmer over low heat for 5 minutes or until thickened.

Veal Scallops with Sherry Sauce

serves three

Ingredients

1	pound veal scallops, pounded thin
	Salt and pepper to taste
½	cup flour
2	tablespoons butter
2	tablespoons olive oil
1	cup beef broth
½	cup chicken broth
⅔	cup dry sherry
2	tablespoons lemon juice
4	cloves of garlic, chopped
½	teaspoon Worcestershire sauce
2	tablespoons minced fresh parsley

▲ Season the veal with salt and pepper and coat with the flour, shaking off the excess. Sauté the veal in the melted butter and olive oil in a heavy skillet over medium-high heat for 1 minute on each side. Transfer to a platter and keep warm. Wipe the skillet with paper towels.

▲ Add the broths, sherry, lemon juice, garlic and Worcestershire sauce to the skillet. Bring to a boil over high heat and cook for 10 minutes or until reduced to ¾ cup. Pour over the veal and garnish with the parsley.

The wood stove had a reservoir holding up to four gallons, where water could be heated to scalding temperature in the course of a day's cooking. Rising from the back… a large warming oven… which provided space to set steaks, biscuits, hotcakes, gravy, or other items that needed to be stockpiled or kept warm while the other cooking proceeded. Under the warming oven at each end was a small iron shelf for the salt box, the grease can, and other items frequently needed.

SALMON RIVER SAGA

Niagara Springs Elk Tenderloin with Caramelized Onions

serves eight

Ingredients

1	elk tenderloin
½	cup vegetable oil
4	teaspoons freshly ground black peppercorns
1	teaspoon salt
1	teaspoon crumbled thyme
½	cup butter
2	large yellow onions, sliced
	Thyme and salt to taste
½	teaspoon sugar
⅔	cup sourmash bourbon

Crispy hash browns and a good zinfandel go well with this dish.

▲ Cut the tenderloin into 1½-inch slices and place in a shallow glass dish. Combine the oil, pepper, 1 teaspoon salt and 1 teaspoon thyme in a bowl and pour over the elk. Marinate for about 30 minutes, turning occasionally.

▲ Melt half the butter in a heavy skillet over medium heat and sauté the onion slices until medium brown. Remove from the skillet and set aside.

▲ Increase the heat and sauté the tenderloin slices in the skillet until medium rare, adding more butter as needed. Remove to a warm platter and keep warm.

▲ Add thyme and salt to taste and sugar to the skillet. Add the bourbon, stirring to deglaze. Return the onions to the skillet and stir to coat. Cook until tender and caramelized. Spoon over the tenderloins and serve immediately.

Burgundy Elk en Croûte

serves twelve

Herb Pastry

1	cup flour
1	teaspoon baking powder
½	teaspoon salt
2	teaspoons sugar
1	tablespoon mixed herbs
3	tablespoons butter
½	cup milk

Elk

3	slices bacon
2	pounds elk steak, 1-inch thick, cubed
½	cup flour
2 to 3	tablespoons olive oil
1	onion, chopped
½	cup carrot chunks
1	cup frozen small whole onions
½	green bell pepper
3	cloves of garlic
1	teaspoon each thyme and rosemary
1	(16-ounce) can tomatoes
1	cup burgundy
2	red potatoes, cubed
8	ounces mushrooms, sliced
1	envelope green peppercorn sauce mix
¼	cup tiny peas
1	egg yolk
1	teaspoon milk

This is a great presentation for elk.

▲ For the pastry, combine the flour, baking powder, salt, sugar and mixed herbs in a medium bowl. Cut in the butter with a fork or pastry blender. Stir in the milk to form a dough.

▲ Knead lightly on a floured surface and roll out to ¼-inch thickness. Cut into leaf shapes with a knife or with special cookie cutters.

▲ For the elk, cook the bacon in a Dutch oven until crisp. Remove and set aside on paper towels. Coat the elk with the flour. Brown in the bacon drippings, adding oil if necessary.

▲ Add the chopped onion and sauté for 3 minutes. Add the carrots, whole onions, green pepper, garlic, thyme, rosemary, tomatoes and burgundy. Simmer for 1 hour. Add the potatoes and mushrooms and cook until tender. Add the peppercorn sauce mix and peas and cook for 15 minutes.

▲ Preheat the oven to 375 degrees. Arrange and overlap the pastry leaves on top of the stew. Whisk together the egg yolk and milk and lightly brush the pastry.

▲ Bake for 30 minutes or until the pastry is golden brown.

Wild Game

Medallions of Venison with Gorgonzola Butter Sauce
serves four

Venison
1	cup olive oil
1	tablespoon freshly ground peppercorns
1	tablespoon chopped garlic
3	tablespoons fresh lemon juice
2	pounds venison backstrap

Gorgonzola Butter Sauce
1	tablespoon minced shallots
¼	cup dry white wine
¼	cup whipping cream
¼	cup crumbled Gorgonzola cheese
½	cup butter, chilled, cut into quarters
½	teaspoon white pepper

▲ For the venison, combine the oil, pepper, garlic and lemon juice in a bowl. Pour over the venison in a dish. Marinate for 1 hour, turning occasionally.

▲ For the sauce, combine the shallots, wine and cream in a saucepan. Cook over medium heat until reduced by ½. Lower the heat and add the crumbled cheese. Cook until melted, stirring to mix well. Whisk in the butter 1 piece at a time. Season with white pepper. Set aside in a warm place, but not over heat, as sauce could separate.

▲ Preheat the grill. Drain the venison.

▲ Grill on a rack close enough to the charcoal or gas flame to allow the oil coating to flare up. Grill to 135 degrees on a meat thermometer or until the outside is charred without overcooking the center. Slice and serve with the sauce.

…the work was hard. Eggs, fruit and vegetables did not fare well on the pack mules over endless miles of trails,…nor did butter and dairy products. Even bacon, a great favorite not only for the meat, but for the bacon grease which made wonderful cooking oil, had lost most of its freshness by the time it arrived in the camps. Therefore, the cooks were more or less limited to the local wild animals, including the deer, bear and other animals killed for food. Bear oil, especially, was good for use as shortening, but not many people wanted to risk tangling with a bear.

FOOTPRINTS ON MOUNTAIN TRAILS

Gallery Six

Poultry and Wild Fowl

Eastern Idaho

This area showcases the rugged spaciousness and pristine splendour of the American West, where some of the finest fly fishing waters on the continent grace the valley floor. Henry's Fork is one of Idaho's 16,000 miles of streams and Mt. Borah, one of over 40 Idaho peaks that top 10,000', rises here at 12,655'. Geyser fed hot water and sand dunes round out a landscape framed by the nearby Grand Teton mountains.

"There are places, high in the mountains, where no man walks for years.
You enter carefully, spilling snow from bent branches.
Pause; watching water drip unto a beaver pond......
A good place to come in early winter."

—Harald Wyndham, Idaho Poet

Summer Night Buffet at Henry's Fork Cabin

Silver Valley Dilled Shrimp, page 22

China Creek Pork Salad, page 60

Silver Creek Spring Trout with Wine and Herbs, page 183

Beef and Asparagus Rolls with Bleu Cheese Sauce, page 119

Lewis and Clark Arugula and Orange Salad, page 43

Green Beans with Balsamic-Glazed Onions, page 90

Sauvignon Blanc - Gewürztraminer - White Zinfandel

Huckleberry Cream Cheese Pie, page 217

or

Lime Fool with Strawberries and Kiwifruit, page 211

Rexburg Chicken Breasts with Balsamic Vinegar

serves two

Ingredients

1	large boneless chicken breast with skin
	Salt and pepper to taste
¼	cup unsalted butter
1	large shallot, minced
3	tablespoons balsamic vinegar
1¾	cups reduced-sodium chicken broth
2	teaspoons minced fresh marjoram

▲ Place a serving platter in an oven preheated to 200 degrees. Rinse the chicken and pat dry; season with salt and pepper.

▲ Melt half the butter in a heavy skillet over high heat. Add the chicken and cook on both sides until crisp. Reduce the heat to medium-low and continue cooking for 8 to 10 minutes or until cooked through and juices run clear. Remove to the heated platter, cover loosely with foil and keep warm in oven.

▲ Drain the skillet and add 1 teaspoon of the butter and the shallot. Sauté for 3 minutes or until the shallot is translucent, stirring the skillet to deglaze. Increase the heat to high and add vinegar. Boil until reduced to a glaze, stirring constantly. Add the broth and boil to reduce to ¼ cup, stirring occasionally. Season with pepper.

▲ Remove the skillet from the heat and whisk in 1 to 2 tablespoons of the butter, the marjoram and any juices from the platter. Taste and adjust the seasonings. Spoon the sauce over the chicken and serve immediately.

Braised Chicken with Mushrooms and Sun-Dried Tomatoes

serves four

Ingredients

2	large whole chicken breasts, cut into halves
	Salt and pepper to taste
1½	tablespoons sun-dried tomato oil
2	small onions, finely chopped
4	large cloves of garlic, minced
1	teaspoon dried basil
½	teaspoon crushed red pepper
16	ounces mushrooms, sliced
1	cup dry red wine
1	cup chicken broth
¼	cup tomato paste
⅔	cup thinly sliced oil-pack sun-dried tomatoes
3	tablespoons minced fresh parsley

▲ Rinse the chicken and pat dry. Season with salt and pepper. Heat the tomato oil in a heavy skillet until hot but not smoking. Add the chicken and cook until brown; transfer to a platter. Sauté the onions, garlic, basil and crushed red pepper in the pan drippings in the skillet over medium-low heat until the onions are tender.

▲ Add the mushrooms and cook over medium heat until softened. Whisk in the wine, broth and tomato paste. Return the chicken to the skillet. Bring to a boil and reduce the heat to a simmer. Cook, covered, for 15 to 20 minutes or until the chicken is cooked through.

▲ Remove the chicken to the platter, cover with foil and keep warm. Add the sun-dried tomatoes to the sauce and simmer for 2 to 3 minutes or until reduced and slightly thickened, whisking constantly. Adjust the seasonings. Add the parsley to the sauce and pour over the chicken. Serve immediately.

Five-Spice Chicken with Cilantro

serves four

Excellent

Ingredients

1	teaspoon cumin
1	teaspoon paprika
½	teaspoon coriander
½	teaspoon ground red pepper
¾	cup plain nonfat yogurt
2	tablespoons fresh lemon juice
1	tablespoon minced fresh ginger
1	teaspoon minced garlic
1	teaspoon salt
1	pound boneless skinless chicken breasts
¼	cup fresh cilantro leaves
4	lemon wedges

This is delicious served with mango chutney.

▲ Combine the cumin, paprika, coriander and pepper in a small saucepan. Cook over low heat for 1 to 2 minutes or until fragrant, stirring constantly.

▲ Combine the seasonings with the yogurt, lemon juice, ginger, garlic and salt in a bowl. Rinse the chicken and pat dry. Add to the marinade, tossing to coat. Marinate at room temperature for 30 minutes or in the refrigerator for 8 hours.

▲ Preheat the broiler and a foil-lined broiler pan. Set the broiler rack 3 inches from the heat source.

▲ Drain the chicken and place in the prepared pan. Broil 3 inches from the heat source for 5 minutes. Turn and broil for another 7 minutes or until the chicken begins to brown. Slice the chicken diagonally across the grain and garnish with the cilantro and lemon wedges.

Lava Hot Springs Chicken and Garlic

serves four

Ingredients

1	chicken, cut into 8 pieces
1	teaspoon salt
¼	teaspoon pepper
1	tablespoon butter
2	tablespoons olive oil
40	large cloves of garlic
½	cup white wine
½	cup chicken broth

▲ Rinse the chicken and pat dry. Season with the salt and pepper. Melt the butter with the oil in a large heavy skillet over medium-high heat. Add the chicken and sauté for 4 minutes on each side or until brown. Drain the skillet.

▲ Reduce the heat to medium and add the garlic cloves, tucking them under the chicken to settle in a layer at the bottom. Sauté for 8 to 10 minutes or until the garlic is light brown, shaking the pan frequently.

▲ Add the wine and broth, stirring to deglaze the skillet. Cover and cook for 10 to 12 minutes or until the juices run clear when a thigh is pricked. Serve the chicken with the garlic and pan juices.

"We raised about 80 chickens this summer. The hawks have bothered them a great deal. Two different times, a hawk took a chicken and carried it a ways but had to let it go. The chickens didn't get hurt. It begins to look bare up here; the hills are brown and the leaves are falling off the trees…the young ones have been teasing to go out all day. Just now, they are regaling themselves with bread and jelly. I made some jelly with silver prunes and some from quince and apples. We got some of those sour apples from the Gross place, and the first jelly I made, I used a third quince juice and the jelly was awful nice. The next two batches were half quince and they both got burned a little."

SALMON RIVER SAGA

Ginger Mustard Chicken

serves three

Ingredients

¼	cup flour
¼	teaspoon salt
¼	teaspoon pepper
3	large boneless skinless chicken breast halves
1	tablespoon butter
¾	cup chicken broth
2	teaspoons minced ginger
1	tablespoon Dijon mustard

This is a good dish for people on a low-cholesterol diet.

▲ Mix the flour, salt and pepper together. Rinse the chicken and pat dry. Coat well with the flour mixture. Sauté in the butter in a large skillet for 8 to 10 minutes or until cooked through. Remove the chicken to a warm platter.

▲ Increase the heat to medium-high and add the chicken broth, stirring to deglaze the skillet. Add the ginger and cook for 2 minutes, stirring constantly. Stir in the mustard. Add the chicken and cook until heated through. Spoon the sauce over the chicken to serve.

Plain ranges were all black iron. All models had heat guard bars across the front and the left end to prevent burning yourself or your clothes if you leaned against the stove. On the fancier models, these…bars and trim…would be of shiny nickel steel…the main body of the stove was black and was refurbished from time to time with a brisk rubdown with stove blacking…the oven had no thermometer, the cook's face serving as a register when the oven door was opened for checking…

SALMON RIVER SAGA

Lookout Mountain Chicken

serves six

Ingredients

6	boneless skinless chicken breasts
¼	cup butter
¼	teaspoon (or more) garlic salt
	Salt and pepper to taste
8	ounces fresh mushrooms, sliced
1	(3-ounce) can French-fried onions
½	cup shredded Monterey Jack cheese

Needs seasoning salt or something else. Actually very good.

Sure to be a family favorite! Quick and easy.

▲ Preheat the oven to 350 degrees. Rinse the chicken and pat dry.

▲ Melt the butter in a large baking dish. Stir in the garlic salt and salt and pepper to taste. Add the chicken and baste on each side with seasoned butter.

▲ Bake, ~~covered~~ *or*, for 1 hour. Add the mushrooms and bake for 15 to 20 minutes longer or until the chicken is tender.

▲ Sprinkle with the *mushrooms* onions and cheese. Bake, uncovered, for 10 to 15 minutes longer or until the cheese melts. Serve immediately.

They raised chickens both for eggs and for cooking. Fruit and vegetables were canned or dried. Chokecherries and currants were usually abundant and excellent for jams, jellies and syrup. Vegetables were traded to their neighbors…for honey. Various kinds of pickles were made, and sauerkraut put up by the gallon.

IDAHO FOLKLIFE: HOMESTEADS TO HEADSTONES

Targhee Pass Chicken Scallops with Mustard Glaze

serves four

Ingredients

4	boneless chicken breasts, trimmed
3	tablespoons flour
½	teaspoon marjoram
½	teaspoon thyme
½	teaspoon pepper
2	tablespoons unsalted butter
½	cup dry vermouth
1	cup chicken broth
2	tablespoons Dijon mustard
¼	teaspoon grated lemon rind
3	tablespoons whipping cream

▲ Rinse the chicken and pat dry. Pound ¼ inch thick between waxed paper. Combine the flour, marjoram, thyme and pepper in a bowl. Reserve 1 tablespoon of the mixture. Coat the chicken with the remaining flour mixture.

▲ Melt the butter in a skillet over medium heat. Add the chicken and brown for 2 minutes on each side. Remove to a plate. Add the vermouth to the skillet and mix with the pan drippings. Boil the mixture for 5 minutes or until reduced to a glaze, stirring to deglaze the skillet. Mix in the chicken broth, mustard and lemon rind. Boil for 2 minutes.

▲ Stir the cream into the reserved flour in a bowl. Whisk in the hot broth from the skillet. Return the mixture to the skillet and simmer for 3 minutes or until thickened and smooth, stirring constantly. Return the chicken to the skillet and cook for 2 minutes longer on each side or until cooked through. Serve immediately.

Soda Springs Chicken and Stuffing

serves six

Ingredients

1	(12-ounce) package stuffing mix
6	chicken breasts
8	ounces Swiss cheese, thinly sliced
1	cup chopped celery
1	(4-ounce) small can sliced mushrooms
1	(10-ounce) can cream of mushroom soup
¾	cup dry white wine
3	tablespoons melted butter

This is one of those easy last-minute recipes that is festive enough for a dinner party.

▲ Preheat the oven to 350 degrees.

▲ Reserve ½ cup of the stuffing mix. Spread the remaining stuffing mix in a greased 9x13-inch baking dish. Rinse the chicken and pat dry. Arrange over the stuffing mix. Top with the cheese slices, celery and mushrooms.

▲ Mix the soup and wine in a bowl and pour over the chicken. Sprinkle with the reserved stuffing and drizzle with the melted butter.

▲ Bake for 45 minutes and serve immediately.

James Wilkins, an English portrait painter, set out in 1849 to create an immense 'moving panorama' of the Oregon Trail…He drew his hazardous descent over the Bear River Mountains into the southeast corner of what is now the Soda Springs area of southern Idaho…

ONE HUNDRED YEARS OF IDAHO ART

Stuffed Chicken Breasts with Roasted Red Pepper Sauce

serves twelve

Chicken

3	small zucchini
	Salt to taste
2	shallots
2	cloves of garlic
1½	(4- to 5-ounce) packages garlic and spice-flavored soft cheese
¾	cup grated Parmesan cheese
12	(6- to 8-ounce) boneless skinless chicken breast halves
	Pepper to taste
¼	cup melted butter
	Paprika to taste

Roasted Red Pepper Sauce

4	large or 8 small red bell peppers
¼	cup raspberry or red wine vinegar
¼	cup dry red wine
2	teaspoons cornstarch
1	cup chicken broth
	Salt and pepper to taste
¼	cup (or more) chicken drippings

▲ For the chicken, preheat the oven to 400 degrees. Shred the zucchini in a food processor. Place in a colander in the sink and sprinkle with salt. Toss well and let stand for 30 minutes. Squeeze a handful at a time in a kitchen towel to remove excess moisture.

▲ Process the shallots and garlic in food processor fitted with a steel blade until minced. Add both cheeses and the zucchini, pulsing until chopped. Rinse the chicken and pat dry. Pound very thin between waxed paper. Sprinkle with salt and pepper. Spread 2 tablespoons of the zucchini mixture evenly over each. Fold one end over, turn in the sides and roll to enclose the filling; secure with a wooden pick or skewer. Arrange in a single layer in a shallow roasting pan.

▲ Baste with the melted butter and sprinkle with paprika. Bake for 25 to 30 minutes or until cooked through, basting once or twice after the first 15 minutes. Remove the skewers and place the chicken on a warm platter. Reserve ¼ to ½ cup drippings.

▲ For the sauce, grill the bell peppers whole or roast in shallow pan under a preheated broiler for 25 to 30 minutes or until the skin is charred, turning frequently. Place in a brown paper bag, close and set aside for 20 minutes. Rub off the skins with the hands. Cut into slices lengthwise, discarding the seeds; do not rinse. Purée in a food processor fitted with a metal blade.

▲ Bring the vinegar and wine to a boil in a medium saucepan. Cook until reduced to ¼ cup. Remove from the heat. Dissolve cornstarch in chicken broth in a small bowl and then whisk into the reduced vinegar mixture. Bring to a boil, whisking constantly. Stir in the red pepper purée and season with salt and pepper. Whisk in the reserved pan drippings.

Idaho Falls Chicken Enchiladas

serves six

Ingredients

1	cup chopped onion
1	clove of garlic, minced
2	tablespoons butter
2	cups chopped cooked chicken breasts
1	(4-ounce) can chopped mild green chiles
½	cup enchilada sauce
½	cup mild salsa
½	teaspoon salt
1	cup whipping cream
12	small flour tortillas
2	cups shredded Cheddar cheese
1	(10-ounce) can cream of chicken soup
1	cup sour cream

▲ Preheat the oven to 350 degrees.

▲ Sauté the onion and garlic in the butter in a skillet until tender. Combine with the chicken, chiles, enchilada sauce, salsa, salt and whipping cream in a bowl. Mix well.

▲ Spray a large skillet with a nonstick cooking spray. Brown each tortilla lightly on both sides in the prepared skillet over medium high heat, spraying the skillet before adding each tortilla to prevent sticking. Stack the tortillas on a plate and set aside.

▲ Spoon some of the chicken mixture along 1 side of each tortilla and roll to enclose the filling. Place seam down in a buttered 9x13-inch baking dish.

▲ Combine the cheese, soup and sour cream in a medium bowl and mix well. Spoon over the enchiladas. The recipe can be prepared up to this point and refrigerated for a few hours; return to room temperature before baking.

▲ Bake, covered with foil, for 30 minutes. Remove foil and continue baking for another 20 minutes or until bubbly. Serve with additional salsa and guacamole.

Blackfoot Chicken and Barley Skillet Supper

serves six

Ingredients

1	pound ground chicken, turkey or beef
½	cup chopped onion
½	cup chopped celery
¼	cup chopped green pepper
1	clove of garlic, minced
2	tablespoons vegetable oil
¾	cup uncooked pearl barley
1	(16-ounce) can tomatoes, cut up
1½	cups water
½	cup chili sauce
1	teaspoon Worcestershire sauce
½	teaspoon marjoram
	Salt and pepper to taste

This quick-to-fix-entrée is sure to please appetites of all ages. Be sure to make enough for second helpings. You may substitute 2 cups chopped uncooked chicken or turkey for the ground poultry or beef. Compliments of the Idaho Barley Commission.

▲ Sauté the chicken, onion, celery, green pepper and garlic in the oil in a heavy skillet for 3 to 4 minutes. Add the barley, tomatoes, water, chili sauce, Worcestershire sauce, marjoram, salt and pepper. Bring to a boil and then reduce the heat to a simmer.

▲ Cover and cook for 1 hour or until the barley is tender and the mixture is of the desired consistency. Adjust the seasonings. Serve immediately.

"Although there is not much to cook, the difficulty and inconvenience of doing it, amounts to a great deal…so by the time one has squatted around the fire and cooked bread and bacon, and made several dozen trips to and from the wagon…washed the dishes (with no place to drain them)…and gotten things ready for an early breakfast, some of the others already have their night caps on."

Helen Carpenter, 1857
WOMEN'S VOICES FROM THE OREGON TRAIL

Fort Hall Turkey Breast Scallopini

serves six

Ingredients

1½	pounds turkey breast, boned, cut into ¼-inch thick slices
¼	cup flour
½	cup butter
8	ounces large mushrooms, cut into quarters
½	cup marsala

The term, scallopini, is usually reserved for veal, but this is a nice adaptation of the traditional dish.

▲ Rinse the turkey and pat dry. Pound ⅛ inch thick between waxed paper. Coat with the flour.

▲ Melt 2 to 3 tablespoons of the butter in a large skillet over medium-high heat until foamy. Add a single layer of the turkey slices. Cook for 1 minute or until light brown on both sides, removing to a warm platter as it browns and adding butter as needed. Repeat with the remaining turkey.

▲ Sauté the mushrooms in the drippings in the skillet until golden brown. Add the wine, stirring to deglaze. Remove to the platter with a slotted spoon.

▲ Bring the wine sauce to a full boil over high heat. Remove from the heat and stir in the remaining butter. Spoon over the turkey and serve immediately.

In 1837, Alfred Jacob Miller was hired by Captain William Drummond Stuart, a Scottish nobleman and adventurer, to illustrate, 'the remarkable scenery and incidents' on an American Fur Company expedition into the far reaches of the West. They traveled nearly to the eastern boundary of what is now Idaho, to the trapper's rendezvous at Green River…

ONE HUNDRED YEARS OF IDAHO ART

Marinated Cornish Hens

serves four

Ingredients

4	Cornish game hens
½	cup soy sauce
¾	cup olive oil
½	cup gin
2	small onions, minced
2	cloves of garlic, minced
¼	teaspoon freshly ground black pepper
⅛	teaspoon crushed red pepper
1	teaspoon ground ginger
1	tablespoon sugar or honey
1	tablespoon Worcestershire sauce

▲ Rinse the hens and pat dry. Place in a large sealable plastic bag. Combine the soy sauce, olive oil, gin, onions, garlic, peppers, ginger, sugar and Worcestershire sauce in a medium bowl. Pour into the bag. Squeeze out excess air and seal. Marinate in the refrigerator overnight.

▲ Preheat the oven to 350 degrees. Drain, reserving the marinade. Place the hens in a roasting pan. Bake for 50 to 60 minutes or until the hens are cooked through and the juices run clear when the thigh is pricked with a knife, basting occasionally with the reserved marinade. Let stand for a few minutes before serving.

"One February day, as I went out my gate to go fishing, my wild chicken ran right up against my feet, and just then I saw the coyote that was trying to get it. So I went back and got my .370 and killed the coyote, and I said, 'that chicken ought to lay us an egg today for saving its hide.' Went on down to Ludwig Rapid and caught a 9-pound steelhead, and when I got back I saw the chicken get off its nest after laying the first egg of the spring. So a good day: a coyote, a steelhead and an egg. Furthermore, our confidence in the chicken was not misplaced."

Sylvan Hart, "Buckskin Bill"
IDAHO LONERS, HERMITS, SOLITARIES, AND INDIVIDUALISTS

American Falls Chukar with Mustard Sauce

serves four

Ingredients

4	whole chukar breasts, cut into halves
¼	cup flour
2	tablespoons butter
1	tablespoon vegetable oil
½	cup dry white wine
½	cup chopped onion
1	clove of garlic, minced
2	cups sliced mushrooms
¾	cup half-and-half
1	teaspoon dry mustard
3	tablespoons Dijon mustard
1	tablespoon prepared mustard
½	teaspoon Worcestershire sauce

This is a favorite recipe from an avid hunter.

▲ Rinse the chukar and pat dry. Pound to flatten slightly and coat with the flour.

▲ Brown in the heated butter and oil in a heavy skillet. Sauté until cooked through. Remove to a platter and keep warm.

▲ Add the wine to the skillet, stirring to deglaze. Add the onion and garlic and cook until translucent. Add the mushrooms and cook until tender.

▲ Whisk the half-and-half, mustards and Worcestershire sauce in a small bowl. Add to the onion mixture and cook over high heat until reduced to the desired consistency. Pour over the chukar and serve immediately.

Henry's Fork Barbecued Duck

serves two

Ingredients

1	cup soy sauce
1	cup lemon juice or white wine
½	cup peanut oil
2	teaspoons garlic powder
4	wild duck quarters or breasts

This is also a good marinade for dove, pigeon or chicken. Serve the duck with a dry white wine or Merlot, scalloped potatoes and a salad.

▲ Combine the soy sauce, lemon juice, oil, and garlic powder in a shallow dish. Rinse the duck and pat dry. Add to the marinade, turning to coat. Marinate at room temperature for 2 hours or in the refrigerator overnight.

▲ Drain, reserving the marinade. Grill the duck over medium-hot coals for 20 to 25 minutes or until cooked through, dipping the duck in the marinade several times; the duck will be black on the outside and medium to medium-rare on the inside.

"I've got six months, from November on, when this place is just like it's always been: nobody visits, and I get my mail twice a month. I pass the winters by doing something all the time. I'd get breakfast, watch otter, work on a gun in the shop. See mountain sheep come in for salt, take a few pictures. Cook supper. Read. That would take care of the whole day."

Sylvan Hart, "Buckskin Bill"
IDAHO LONERS, HERMITS, SOLITARIES, AND INDIVIDUALISTS

Marinated Duck with Port Sauce

serves eight

Marinated Duck

1½	cups dry red wine
½	cup balsamic vinegar
3	tablespoons soy sauce
½	cup fresh lemon juice
4	cloves of garlic, minced
½	cup olive oil
1	tablespoon grated fresh ginger
	Salt and pepper to taste
2	(2-pound) boneless duck breasts with skin or 2 wild ducks

Port Sauce

3	tablespoons sugar
3	tablespoons water
2	tablespoons white wine vinegar
¼	cup balsamic vinegar
½	cup minced shallots
2	large cloves of garlic, minced
2	tablespoons butter or duck fat
1¾	cups dry red wine
¾	cup beef broth
½	cup whipping cream
½	cup tawny port
3	tablespoons flour
¼	cup unsalted butter, softened

▲ For the marinated duck, combine the wine, vinegar, soy sauce, lemon juice, garlic, oil, ginger, salt and pepper in a large sealable plastic bag. Rinse the duck and pat dry. Add the duck to the bag, squeeze out excess air, seal and mix well to coat. Marinate in the refrigerator for 8 hours.

▲ Drain the duck and pat dry. Score the skin at 1-inch intervals in a crisscross pattern, taking care not to cut through the fat into the meat. Season with salt and pepper.

▲ Preheat the oven to 450 degrees. Heat 2 ovenproof skillets over medium-high heat and add 1 duck breast skin side down to each skillet. Cook for 10 minutes, turn and cook for 2 minutes longer. Place skillets in the oven and roast the duck for 5 to 7 minutes or until cooked through, reserving any pan drippings.

▲ For the sauce, bring the sugar and water to a boil in a heavy saucepan, stirring to dissolve the sugar. Boil until the mixture is a caramel color. Gradually stir in the vinegars.

▲ Sauté the shallots and garlic in 2 tablespoons butter in a skillet over medium heat until tender. Add the dry red wine and boil until the mixture is reduced by ½. Add the beef broth and boil until the mixture is reduced by ⅓. Press the mixture through a fine sieve into the vinegar mixture in the saucepan.

▲ Whisk in the cream and port wine and simmer for 1 minute. Blend the flour and unsalted butter in a small bowl and add to the sauce. Cook until thickened, stirring constantly. Add any reserved pan juices from the duck.

▲ Slice the duck diagonally across the grain into thin slices. Arrange on a warm serving platter and serve with the sauce.

Camas Duck Breasts with Walnut Salad

serves six

Grilled Duck

4	duck breasts
1	tablespoon sunflower oil

Salad

12	small escarole leaves or curly endive
12	radicchio leaves
12	tiny sprigs watercress
1	head Belgian endive, outer leaves removed
½	cup coarsely chopped walnuts

Walnut Oil Dressing

1½	tablespoons white wine vinegar
1½	tablespoons lemon juice
3	tablespoons walnut oil
3	tablespoons sunflower oil

This is a great light first course for a dinner party.

▲ For the grilled duck, heat the grill or broiler to moderate heat. Rinse the duck, pat dry and rub with the oil. Grill skin side up for 6 to 8 minutes. Turn and grill for 4 to 5 minutes longer or until cooked through. Cool for 30 minutes. Cut diagonally into slices and arrange on serving plates.

▲ For the salad, arrange the escarole, radicchio, watercress and endive beside the duck; sprinkle with the walnuts.

▲ For the dressing, combine the vinegar and lemon juice and then slowly whisk in oils. Drizzle over the duck and salad and serve slightly warm.

Pocatello Pheasant Au Vin

serves six

Ingredients

2	pheasant or chukar
6	whole cloves
1	bay leaf, crushed
1	onion, thinly sliced
1	teaspoon dried sage, crushed
1	bottle port or red wine
½	cup flour
¼	cup butter
1	cup sour cream

This is delicious served with a wild rice mix.

▲ Rinse the pheasant and pat dry. Cut into serving pieces and place in a shallow dish. Combine the cloves, bay leaf, onion and sage with enough port to cover the pheasant. Cover and marinate in the refrigerator for 12 hours.

▲ Drain the pheasant and reserve the liquid. Pat dry and coat with the flour.

▲ Preheat the oven to 300 degrees. Heat an ovenproof skillet on the stove top and melt the butter. Add the pheasant and brown on both sides. Remove from the heat.

▲ Strain the marinade over the pheasant. Bake, covered, for 1 to 1½ hours, stirring the sour cream into the skillet during the last 30 minutes and baking uncovered if necessary to thicken the sauce.

Very good

Wild Fowl

Fort Henry Cinnamon Pheasant

serves two

Ingredients

1	pheasant
	Cinnamon to taste
2	tablespoons minced chives
	Pepper to taste
	Fines herbes or Beau Monde seasoning to taste
3	tablespoons butter
12	juniper berries (optional)
4	shallots, finely chopped
1 to 2	cups onion soup or cream soup
1	cup dry white wine
2	tablespoons Scotch (optional)

can has (with water) 2 c

▲ Preheat the oven to 325 degrees. Rinse the pheasant and pat dry. Rub generously inside and out with cinnamon. Sprinkle with the chives, pepper and *fines herbes*.

▲ Heat a Dutch oven on the stove top and melt the butter. Brown the pheasant on all sides in the butter. Add the juniper berries, shallots and 1 cup soup.

▲ Roast in the oven for 1½ hours, basting regularly with the white wine and adding additional soup if needed for the desired consistency.

▲ Remove the pheasant from the Dutch oven and cut into 4 pieces. Return to the Dutch oven and roast for 30 minutes longer. Pour the whiskey over the pheasant and ignite if desired. Serve on a bed of white or wild rice.

Within ten years of Lewis and Clark's venture, the first American fur post west of the Rocky Mountains was founded at Fort Henry on the headwaters of the Snake River. By the time missionaries entered the area in the 1830s, the Rock Mountain Fur Company and the Hudson Bay Company had established trading posts in the region of present-day southern Idaho…

ONE HUNDRED YEARS OF IDAHO ART

Breast of Pheasant with Fresh Sage

serves four

Ingredients

4	pheasant breasts, boned
2	cups flour
	Salt and pepper to taste
¼	cup butter
10	fresh sage leaves
2	tablespoons tomato paste
2	tablespoons brandy
1	cup whipping cream

Serve this with a good Sauvignon Blanc.

▲ Preheat the oven to 200 degrees and warm an ovenproof platter. Rinse the pheasant and pat dry. Coat with a mixture of the flour, salt and pepper.

▲ Heat a large heavy skillet and melt the butter. Cook the pheasant on both sides until cooked through, taking care not to overbrown. Remove to the platter, cover with foil and keep warm in oven.

▲ Increase the heat under the skillet and add the sage leaves and tomato paste. Add the brandy, stirring to deglaze. Add the cream and stir briskly to mix well. Cook until the sauce is reduced to the desired consistency. Taste and adjust the seasonings. Pour over the pheasant.

Wild Fowl

Minnetonka Cave Pheasant Strips

serves four

Ingredients

2	whole pheasant breasts
⅓	(or more) cup plain bread crumbs
2	tablespoons butter
2	tablespoons vegetable oil
2	tablespoons sweet vermouth
1	teaspoon soy sauce
2	teaspoons lemon juice
	Several sprigs of fresh parsley or watercress

▲ Rinse the pheasant and pat dry. Cut across the grain into ½-inch wide strips and roll in the bread crumbs.

▲ Melt the butter with the oil in a heavy skillet over medium heat. Sauté the pheasant for 3 minutes on each side or until cooked through.

▲ Combine the vermouth, soy sauce and lemon juice and pour into the skillet. Bring to a boil and cook just until the sauce thickens. Top with the parsley.

No boundaries existed for the state of Idaho when explorers, mountain men, missionaries, and immigrants first considered making the long trek west. Located beyond the far reaches of the Rocky Mountains, Idaho was yet to be systematically explored at the beginning of the nineteenth century. Its terrain was difficult to penetrate, inhabited by Indians, and reported to have unusual geologic characteristics quite unlike geographic features found in the East. Early written accounts emphasized the exotic nature of the country, with its vast and spectacular landscapes and fascinating native population.

ONE HUNDRED YEARS OF IDAHO ART

Gallery Seven

Seafood

Central Idaho Rockies

The Central Rockies encompass a vast arena of sunshine, snow, ice skaters, skiers and golfers, and are surrounded by a valley of starry nights and clear sparkling air. It is a place that author Ernest Hemingway called his own and it ultimately became his final resting place. While Idaho has remained a well guarded secret, the Central Rockies became, in 1936, the home of America's first destination ski resort; a resort of casual sophistication, fine restaurants, and a haven for artists and galleries. Ketchum, Sun Valley, Hailey and the entire Wood River Valley is a sparkling diamond in a pair of blue jeans.

"There's a Big Wood River, there's a Silver Creek
There's a Copper Basin wide and deep
There's a Baldy Mountain, there's a Warm Springs Line
And a wide blue sky where the sun shines most o' the time."
                                        —John Huckins, UP IN IDAHO

Sun Valley New Year's Eve Dinner

Star Garnet Gougere Wreath, page 17
Champagne

Trail Creek Balsamic Glazed Salmon, page 179
Gewürztraminer

Garden Valley Chilled Pea Soup, page 70
Chardonnay

Marinated Duck with Port Sauce, page 168

Silver City Wild Rice, page 109

Broccoli with Pine Nuts and Raisins, page 92
Pinot Noir Reserve

Port and Stilton Salad, page 52

Custard Tart with Sautéed Pears, page 220
Late Harvest Riesling

Ernest Hemingway's Trout

serves six

Ingredients

6	slices bacon
3	green onions, chopped
1	tablespoon chopped fresh parsley
2	tablespoons lemon juice
¼	teaspoon pepper
6	(8-ounce) trout, cleaned
	Seasoned salt to taste
½	cup buttermilk baking mix
2	tablespoons yellow cornmeal
6	lemon wedges

"A pan of fried trout can't be bettered," wrote Ernest Hemingway. "But there is a good and bad way of frying them." The good way, according to an article Hemingway wrote for the Toronto Star in 1920, is to coat them with cornmeal and then cook them slowly in bacon drippings until crisp outside but still moist inside. This recipe combines the cornmeal with baking mix for an extra-crispy coating.

▲ Fry the bacon in a large skillet over medium heat until crisp. Drain and reserve 2 to 3 tablespoons drippings in the skillet.

▲ Combine the onions, parsley, lemon juice and pepper in a bowl. Sprinkle the trout cavities with seasoned salt and fill with the onion mixture. Coat with a mixture of the baking mix and cornmeal.

▲ Fry the trout ½ at a time in the reserved bacon drippings for 4 to 5 minutes on each side or until the fish flakes easily. Top with the bacon to serve and garnish with the lemon wedges.

Best of all he loved the fall. The leaves yellow on the cottonwoods, leaves floating on the trout streams and above the hills, the high, blue, windless skies. Now he will be part of them forever.

Ernest Hemingway Memorial at Trail Creek, Sun Valley, Idaho

Excellent

Moo Shu Salmon

serves four

6 to 8	dried or fresh shiitake mushrooms
12	(6-ounce) flour tortillas
1	(12-ounce) salmon fillet
1	tablespoon soy sauce
1	tablespoon sesame oil
2	tablespoons vegetable oil
1 or 2	slices fresh ginger
3	eggs, lightly beaten
4	green onions, cut into 1-inch pieces
3	cloves of garlic, minced
1	tablespoon minced fresh ginger
3	cups finely shredded cabbage
1	(8-ounce) can bamboo shoots, slivered
2	tablespoons water
1/3	cup hoisin sauce, plum sauce or duck sauce

The is a unique twist on a popular Chinese dish. It can also be made with snapper, sea bass, swordfish, tuna or shrimp. Chinese "pancakes" are made with rice flour and are thinner than tortillas. They can sometimes be found frozen in Asian markets. Flour tortillas work just as well and are actually handier for eating out of hand.

▲ Preheat the oven to 350 degrees. Soak dried mushrooms in hot water in a bowl for 30 minutes. Drain, squeeze out excess moisture, discard the stems and slice into thin strips.

▲ Rinse the salmon and pat dry. Cut crosswise into ¼-inch slices. Mix the soy sauce and sesame oil in a small bowl and set aside.

▲ Heat 2 teaspoons vegetable oil in a wok or skillet over medium heat and add the ginger slices. Stir-fry for several seconds. Add the eggs and cook until soft-set, stirring to break into pieces. Remove to a bowl, discarding the ginger.

▲ Add 1 teaspoon vegetable oil and the salmon to the wok. Stir-fry just until cooked through. Remove to the bowl. Add the remaining vegetable oil and the green onions, garlic and minced ginger to the wok. Stir-fry over medium heat for 30 seconds. Add the mushrooms. Stir-fry for 30 seconds. Add the cabbage, bamboo shoots and a small amount of water if needed. Stir-fry until the cabbage is wilted.

▲ Return the egg and salmon to the wok and add the sesame oil mixture; toss to mix well. Cook until heated through.

▲ Wrap the tortillas in foil and heat in the oven for 15 minutes or until heated through. Spoon the salmon mixture onto the tortillas and roll to enclose. Serve with the hoisin sauce.

Good

Trail Creek Balsamic-Glazed Salmon

serves six

Ingredients

4	teaspoons thinly sliced garlic
1	tablespoon olive oil
4	teaspoons Dijon mustard
1	tablespoon honey
⅓	cup balsamic vinegar
1	tablespoon olive oil
	Salt and freshly ground pepper to taste
6	(5-ounce) salmon fillets
2	tablespoons julienned fresh basil leaves
3	sprigs of basil

Bill loves it

The flavor of the basil complements the flavor of the salmon in this dish.

▲ Preheat the oven to 475 degrees.

▲ Sauté the garlic in 1 tablespoon olive oil in a medium saucepan over medium heat for 3 minutes. Add the mustard, honey, vinegar, remaining 1 tablespoon olive oil, salt and pepper and mix well. Simmer for 3 minutes or until slightly thickened.

▲ Rinse the salmon and pat dry. Arrange in a single layer in a foil-lined baking pan. Brush with some of the warm glaze. Bake for 10 to 14 minutes or until cooked through.

▲ Remove the salmon to a warm platter and brush with the remaining glaze. Top with the basil.

Make ½ recipe – can use more sauce

Excitement ran high as the annual salmon run began. The men labored from dawn to dusk with spear, net and trap, heaping the beaches high with fat fish, which the women cleaned, dried, and smoked. With their stores of dried salmon and roots, the Nez Perce seldom suffered famine as did many of the tribes.

NATIVE FOODS USED BY THE NEZ PERCE INDIANS OF IDAHO

Summer Salmon and Corn Relish with Basil Vinaigrette

serves four

Basil Vinaigrette

½	cup balsamic vinegar
½	cup red wine vinegar
½	cup packed chopped fresh basil
1	tablespoon minced garlic
2	teaspoons Asian red chile paste with garlic
½	cup olive oil

Corn Relish

3	cups cooked corn kernels
½	cup chopped green bell pepper
½	cup chopped red bell pepper
¼	cup chopped black olives
½	cup chopped red onion
	Salt and pepper to taste

Salmon

4	(6-ounce) salmon fillets
8 to 10	cups mixed salad greens
2	large firm tomatoes, thickly sliced

▲ For the basil vinaigrette, combine the balsamic vinegar, wine vinegar, basil, garlic and chile paste in a blender or food processor and process until smooth. Add the olive oil gradually, processing constantly until well mixed. Use immediately or chill for up to 2 days.

▲ For the corn relish, combine the corn, bell peppers, olives and onion in a bowl. Add ⅓ cup of the basil vinaigrette and mix well. Season with salt and pepper. Chill for up to 4 hours.

▲ For the salmon, rinse the fillets and pat dry. Arrange in a single layer in a 9x13-inch baking dish. Drizzle with ¾ cup of the basil vinaigrette. Marinate in the refrigerator for 1 to 8 hours, turning every 15 minutes.

▲ Prepare the grill and spread the coals in a single layer; coals are ready when the hand can be held at grill level for 3 to 4 seconds. Spray the grill rack with nonstick cooking spray. Drain the salmon and grill for 8 to 10 minutes or until opaque in the thickest portion but still moist, turning after 4 minutes. Remove to a warm platter and cover with foil.

▲ Mix the salad greens with the remaining basil vinaigrette in a bowl and toss lightly. Arrange on 4 serving plates. Arrange the corn relish and tomato slices on 1 side. Place the salmon fillet on the top and serve immediately.

River Run Herbed Sole Fillets

serves two

Ingredients

2	tablespoons butter
1	tablespoon olive oil
⅛	teaspoon onion salt
⅛	teaspoon dried oregano
⅛	teaspoon dried parsley
⅛	teaspoon dried tarragon
⅛	teaspoon pepper
½	teaspoon minced garlic
1	pound sole fillets
2 to 3	tablespoons dry sherry

▲ Melt the butter with the olive oil in a large skillet over medium heat. Stir in the onion salt, oregano, parsley, tarragon, pepper and garlic. Sauté for 1 minute. Reduce the heat to low and add the fish.

▲ Cook for 5 to 6 minutes or until the fish flakes easily, turning after 3 minutes; do not overcook. Remove the fish to a heated platter and cover with foil to keep warm.

▲ Add the sherry to the skillet, stirring to deglaze. Cook over high heat for 30 to 45 seconds. Pour over the fish and serve immediately.

While the railroad helped open access to northern Idaho, and the Oregon Trail served the south, the rugged central mountains still made travel difficult between these two regions of the state. Steep mountains and river canyons, transecting the central portion of the territory, forbade passage to all but those hardy individuals willing to tackle the rough terrain by foot or on horseback. Some of these were itinerant artists who, beginning in the 1880s, crisscrossed the state to make their livelihood...

ONE HUNDRED YEARS OF IDAHO ART

Wood River Sole and Cabbage with Mustard Butter Sauce

serves two

Ingredients

4	cups thinly sliced cabbage
	Salt to taste
1½	tablespoons Dijon mustard
1	tablespoon white wine vinegar
1	tablespoon dry sherry
8	ounces sole or flounder fillets
½	cup milk
3	tablespoons flour
	Pepper to taste
¼	cup vegetable oil
3	tablespoons butter
2	green onions, sliced

▲ Preheat the oven to 200 degrees.

▲ Cook the cabbage in salted boiling water in a saucepan for 1 minute; drain. Remove to a platter, cover with foil and place in the warm oven.

▲ Whisk the mustard, vinegar and sherry in a small bowl and set aside.

▲ Dip the fish fillets into the milk and then coat with a mixture of the flour, salt and pepper, shaking off the excess. Sauté in the heated vegetable oil in a large skillet for 2 to 3 minutes or until the fish flakes easily; drain. Arrange over the cabbage.

▲ Drain the skillet and wipe with a paper towel. Add the butter to the skillet and heat until light brown and the foam subsides. Whisk in the mustard mixture. Cook until heated through. Spoon over the fish and cabbage. Top with the green onions.

Evening is the time to visit the riverbank. Not fishing, but just to walk among the boulders, looking at forget-me-not plants spreading over the sand . . . and then it is time to return to the house to shut the chicken house, so night-prowling varmints can't get in...The woodbox was filled before you went to the riverbank, so there are only the lamps to light before building a fire in the cookstove so supper for you and the little dog can be cooked. It is a nice world, this canyon of the Salmon.

Lydia Frances Coyle, Shoup, Idaho
IDAHO LONERS, HERMITS, SOLITARIES, AND INDIVIDUALISTS

Silver Creek Spring Trout with Wine and Herbs
serves four

Ingredients

¼	cup olive oil
	Juice of 1 lemon
1	teaspoon dried thyme
4	cloves of garlic, minced
	Salt and pepper to taste
4	(8-ounce) whole trout, filleted with heads and tails removed
½	cup dry white wine

Trout is an economical fish with a delicate flavor, and this recipe uses it to good advantage.

▲ Preheat the broiler. Mix the olive oil, lemon juice, thyme, garlic, salt and pepper in a small bowl.

▲ Place the fish skin side down in a large ovenproof skillet, spreading the fish open in a butterflied position. Drizzle with half the oil mixture.

▲ Broil for 3 minutes or until the fillets are slightly opaque but not cooked through. Remove to the stove top.

▲ Stir the wine into the remaining oil mixture. Add to the hot skillet, basting the fish well. Cook for 3 minutes longer or until the fish flakes easily.

Life at Fort Boise, the Oregon Trail, according to Idaho State Historian Dr. Merle Wells:
…how they grew two acres of turnips, cabbages and beets; raised 2,000 sheep and 75 pigs, and how they dined on salmon, sturgeon, duck and elk provided by a dozen staff hunters…

IDAHO WOMEN IN HISTORY

Good meal

Seafood

Sautéed Fish with Roasted Red Bell Pepper Sauce

serves two

Roasted Red Bell Pepper Sauce

— Lots of sauce — could make ½

3	medium red bell peppers
2 or 3	sun-dried tomatoes
1½	teaspoons finely minced garlic
½	cup unseasoned rice vinegar
2	tablespoons cider vinegar
1	tablespoon sugar
1	teaspoon salt
½ to 1	teaspoon sesame oil
½	teaspoon chile-infused oil

Fish

⅓	cup soy sauce
1	teaspoon minced fresh ginger
¼	cup Chinese rice wine or dry sherry
1	teaspoon sugar
½	teaspoon sesame oil
2	scallions, sliced
1	tablespoon vegetable oil
1	pound fresh fish steaks
1 to 2	tablespoons chopped chives

Choose from swordfish, sea bass, tuna or halibut for this dish.

▲ For the sauce, roast the bell peppers on a grill or in a 500-degree oven until they are blistered and charred. Place in a non-recycled paper bag or covered bowl and let stand for 30 minutes. Rub off the peels and chop, discarding the seeds; do not rinse.

▲ Cover the sun-dried tomatoes with hot water in a bowl and let stand for 30 minutes or until softened. Drain and chop.

▲ Combine the peppers and tomatoes in a food processor and process until nearly smooth. Add the garlic and pulse to mix. Combine the vinegars, sugar and salt in a bowl and mix well. Add to the food processor and mix. Combine the sesame oil and infused oil and add to the food processor gradually, processing constantly until smooth. Adjust seasonings.

▲ For the fish, combine the soy sauce, ginger, rice wine, sugar, sesame oil and scallions in a bowl and whisk to mix well. Pour over the fish in a shallow dish and marinate for 15 minutes, turning once.

▲ Heat a heavy-bottomed skillet over high heat until a drop of water sizzles. Add the vegetable oil and swirl to coat well. Heat until the oil is nearly smoking. Add the fish and pan-fry for 3 to 4 minutes or until the fish flakes easily, turning once.

▲ Remove to heated serving plates and spoon the sauce over the top. Sprinkle with the chives.

Linguini with Clam Sauce

serves four

Ingredients

3	(6-ounce) cans chopped clams
2	tablespoons chopped fresh parsley
2	tablespoons chopped green onions
3	cloves of garlic, chopped
1	teaspoon oregano
½	cup butter
6	tablespoons dry vermouth
1	teaspoon salt
1	teaspoon pepper
	Cayenne pepper to taste
12	ounces uncooked pasta

This is one of the easiest and most delicious pastas you can make.

▲ Drain 1 can of the clams.

▲ Sauté the parsley, green onions, garlic and oregano in the butter in a skillet until the green onions are tender. Add the wine, clams, salt and pepper. Simmer for 5 minutes.

▲ Cook the pasta al dente using the package directions; drain. Add the clam sauce and toss to mix well. Serve immediately.

As to a diet suited to the plains, very many who cross seem to think that none of the luxuries of home can be enjoyed in a trip of this kind. From this fact they provide themselves with only breadstuffs and meats, while fruit, butter and eggs are left quite out of the bill. We have observed a very great difference in the health of the parties. Those who use meats and little or no fruit, incline to the scurvy, while those who use fruits and very little bacon or meat, never have it.

BOUND FOR IDAHO

Mussels with Plum Tomatoes

serves four

Ingredients

4	pounds mussels, scrubbed, debearded
2½	cups chopped seeded plum tomatoes
6	scallions, chopped
8	ounces mushrooms, coarsely chopped
2	onions, coarsely chopped
8	cloves of garlic, sliced
1	cup dry white wine
¼	cup virgin olive oil
1½	teaspoons Tabasco sauce
	Salt to taste
¼	cup coarsely chopped fresh parsley

This is the simplest way to cook mussels: all the ingredients are combined in a saucepan and the mixture is cooked together for a few minutes. There is enough juice in the mussels, mushrooms and tomatoes to create a nice sauce. Serve it for casual dining or as a first course.

▲ Combine the mussels, tomatoes, scallions, mushrooms, onions, garlic, wine, olive oil, Tabasco sauce and salt in a large saucepan and bring to a boil. Cook, covered, for 6 to 7 minutes or until the mussels open, stirring occasionally. Discard any that do not open.

▲ Spoon the mussels into 4 large serving bowls and spoon the sauce over the top. Sprinkle with the parsley.

In spring, summer, and autumn, the climate is delightful; the days are never sultry and the nights are cool. The winters on the high mountains are accompanied with extreme cold and heavy snow.

IDAHO TERRITORY 1881

Elkhorn Baked Scallops
serves six

Ingredients

6	tablespoons butter
1	pound bay scallops
1	teaspoon salt
	Pepper to taste
1½	cups unsalted cracker crumbs
½	cup soft bread crumbs
½	cup heavy cream

▲ Preheat the oven to 350 degrees and butter 6 individual shells or ramekins. Season the scallops with salt and pepper.

▲ Melt the butter in a skillet over medium heat. Heat until the foam subsides and stir in the cracker crumbs. Sauté for 4 or 5 minutes or until golden brown. Stir in the bread crumbs.

▲ Spoon half the crumb mixture into the prepared baking dishes. Add the scallops and pour the cream over the scallops. Top with the remaining crumb mixture.

▲ Bake for 30 minutes or until golden brown.

With the possibility of living at any desired elevation above sea level; with a rarified, dry, pure atmosphere; with almost constantly bright, genial sunshine; with a light, dry, soil, and with an abundance of pure water fresh from mountain streams or medicinal waters from numerous springs, is it any wonder that Idaho is the healthiest region in America?

IDAHO TERRITORY 1881

Pasta with Scallops and Tarragon
serves four

Ingredients

½	cup finely chopped yellow onion
2	tablespoons olive oil
1	(32-ounce) can Italian plum tomatoes, drained, chopped
2	teaspoons tarragon
	Salt and pepper to taste
1	cup heavy cream
1½	cups scallops
	Cayenne pepper to taste
4	quarts water
2	tablespoons salt
16	ounces uncooked angel hair pasta or spaghetti

This is hearty enough for a main course, but it also makes a beautiful first course for an elegant dinner.

▲ Cook the onion, covered, in the heated olive oil in a saucepan over low heat for 25 minutes or until tender. Add the tomatoes, tarragon and salt and pepper to taste. Bring to a boil and reduce the heat. Simmer, covered, for 30 minutes, stirring occasionally.

▲ Cool the mixture slightly and pureé it in a food processor or food mill. Return to the saucepan and stir in the cream. Simmer over medium heat for 15 minutes or until slightly reduced, stirring frequently. Adjust the seasonings.

▲ Add the scallops and cayenne pepper. Simmer for 3 to 5 minutes or until the scallops are cooked through.

▲ Bring the water and 2 tablespoons salt to a boil in a large saucepan. Add the pasta and cook al dente; drain.

▲ Spoon the pasta onto serving plates and top with the scallop sauce. Garnish with parsley, basil or tarragon.

Baker Creek Cabin Shrimp

serves six

Ingredients

1¼	cups chopped onions
½	cup chopped celery
2	tablespoons vegetable oil
2	tomatoes, peeled, chopped
2	teaspoons salt
¼	teaspoon crushed red pepper
½	bay leaf
½	cup ketchup
2	pounds uncooked shrimp, peeled, deveined
½	cup hot water
½	cup chunky peanut butter

You may substitute one and one-half pounds cooked chicken for the shrimp if desired.

▲ Sauté the onions and celery in the heated oil in a skillet over low heat until tender but not brown.

▲ Add the tomatoes, salt, red pepper, bay leaf and ketchup and mix well. Simmer, covered, for 15 minutes. Add the shrimp, water and peanut butter. Simmer, covered, for 10 minutes longer. Discard the bay leaf. Serve over rice.

Artists who accompanied the surveys and exploratory expeditions generally worked in pencil, ink, or watercolor, mediums that were especially appropriate for rough working conditions. For artists journeying by wagon or horseback, watercolor was particularly well suited.

ONE HUNDRED YEARS OF IDAHO ART

Baldy Shrimp and Scallop Sauté

serves six

Ingredients

6	large cloves of garlic, minced
3	tablespoons butter
3	tablespoons olive oil
16	ounces mushrooms, sliced
2	tablespoons tomato paste or salsa
¼	cup dry white wine
¼	cup lemon juice
1	pound shrimp, peeled, deveined
1	bunch green onions, sliced
1	pound scallops
	Salt and pepper to taste
⅓	cup chopped fresh parsley

▲ Sauté the garlic in the heated butter and olive oil in a large heavy skillet over medium heat for 1 minute. Increase the heat to high and add the mushrooms. Sauté for 5 minutes or until tender.

▲ Stir in the tomato paste, white wine and lemon juice and bring to a boil. Add the shrimp and green onions. Cook for 1 minute, stirring constantly. Add the scallops. Cook for 3 minutes or until the seafood is cooked through.

▲ Season with salt and pepper. Sprinkle with parsley and serve over rice.

As high as 10,000 feet spots are found covered with luxuriant grass and alpine flowers, and surrounded by dense forests of fir, spruce, and pine. The sky is usually free from clouds, and sunshiny days are the rule.

IDAHO TERRITORY 1881

Sun Valley Skiers Shrimp

serves four

Ingredients

1	pound large uncooked shrimp, peeled, deveined, butterflied
¼	cup cooking sherry or rice wine
1	tablespoon grated fresh ginger
½	cup chicken broth
2	tablespoons soy sauce
2	tablespoons ketchup
1	tablespoon cornstarch
1	tablespoon rice vinegar or white wine vinegar
1	tablespoon sugar
1	teaspoon sesame oil
¼	teaspoon cayenne pepper
4	teaspoons peanut oil
3	bunches watercress, stemmed
2	red bell peppers, cut into 1-inch squares
2	cloves of garlic, minced
8	green onions, sliced diagonally into 1-inch pieces

This dish makes a colorful and fragrant presentation. It has just a hint of spice, but not enough to mask the flavors. Substitute spinach if you cannot find fresh watercress, but you'll miss the peppery flavor.

▲ Toss the shrimp with half the sherry and ginger in a bowl. Marinate in the refrigerator for 30 minutes or longer.

▲ Mix the remaining sherry with the chicken broth, soy sauce, ketchup, cornstarch, rice vinegar, sugar, sesame oil and cayenne pepper in a bowl and set aside.

▲ Heat half the peanut oil in a wok or heavy skillet. Add the watercress and stir-fry for 1 minute or until wilted. Remove with a slotted spoon and arrange around the edge of a serving platter or 4 serving plates.

▲ Add the remaining peanut oil and the bell peppers and garlic to the wok. Stir-fry for 1 minute over medium heat. Increase the heat and add the shrimp and green onions. Stir-fry for 1 to 2 minutes or until the shrimp turn pink, adding additional oil if needed. Stir the sherry mixture and add to the wok. Cook until thickened and clear, stirring constantly.

▲ Spoon onto the prepared platter or plates and serve immediately.

Pasta with Shrimp, Tomatoes and Arugula

serves four

Ingredients

16	ounces uncooked fettucini or spaghetti
¼	cup olive oil
1	pound (24-count) shrimp, peeled, deveined
4	large cloves of garlic, minced
	Crushed red pepper to taste
2	onions, finely chopped
5	plum tomatoes, chopped
	Salt and pepper to taste
1	cup dry white wine
1	cup chicken broth
⅓	cup heavy cream
2	bunches arugula, chopped
¼	cup minced fresh parsley

Substitute fresh spinach if fresh arugula is not available for this dish.

▲ Cook the pasta al dente using the package directions; drain and keep warm.

▲ Heat the oil in a heavy skillet over medium-high heat until hot but not smoking. Add the shrimp, garlic and red pepper and sauté for 1 to 2 minutes or until the shrimp turn pink; do not allow the garlic to overbrown. Remove to a bowl with a slotted spoon.

▲ Add the onions, tomatoes, salt and pepper to the skillet. Sauté until the vegetables are tender. Add the wine and cook until the mixture is reduced by ½. Add the broth and cook until the mixture is again reduced by ½. Stir in the cream and cook until slightly thickened.

▲ Add the arugula and shrimp. Cook for 1 minute or until the shrimp is heated through. Stir in the parsley, salt and pepper.

▲ Combine with the hot pasta in a serving bowl and toss to mix well.

Seattle Ridge Seafood and Mushroom Casserole
serves eight

Ingredients

8	ounces cream cheese
½	cup butter
1	pound medium uncooked shrimp, peeled, deveined
1	large onion, chopped
1	green bell pepper, chopped
2	stalks celery, chopped
2	tablespoons butter
1	(10-ounce) can cream of mushroom soup
1	(8-ounce) can mushrooms, drained
1	tablespoon garlic salt
1	teaspoon Tabasco sauce
½	teaspoon crushed red pepper
2	cups crab meat, picked, rinsed
¾	cup cooked rice
1	cup shredded sharp Cheddar cheese
½	cup cracker crumbs

Serve this with a green salad, garlic bread and bread pudding with rum sauce for a meal with a Cajun flavor.

▲ Preheat the oven to 350 degrees and butter a 2-quart baking dish.

▲ Melt the cream cheese with ½ cup butter in a double boiler, stirring to blend well; set aside.

▲ Sauté the shrimp, onion, bell pepper and celery in 2 tablespoons butter in a large skillet. Remove from the heat and stir in the cream cheese mixture. Add the soup, mushrooms, garlic salt, Tabasco sauce, red pepper, crab meat and rice and mix well.

▲ Spoon into the baking dish and top with the cheese and cracker crumbs. Bake for 20 to 30 minutes or until bubbly.

Gallery Eight
Desserts

Northeast Idaho

The Sawtooth basin has some of Idaho's most photographed and spectacular scenery. The White Cloud Mountains and terra cotta Sawtooth mountains tower above a lush valley where the head waters of the Salmon River and sparkling lakes combine with high alpine meadows to create a profound tribute to nature's artistry. From the whisper of falling snow to the brilliant wild-flowers in the warm, spring sun, N.E. Idaho will cast it's spell.

"My cabin door looks out upon
A rugged mountain side where pines
Grow from the rocks and at its base
A river, banked with boulders winds…

When morning rays gleam from above
The towering peaks, white-capped with snow,
What lavish beauty Nature showers
Upon these hills of Idaho."

—*Della Adams Leitner*
WHITE GOLD POEMS

Sunset Dessert Buffet on an Idaho Mountain Ranch

Redfish Lake Chocolate Devil with Raspberry Sauce, page 199

Sawtooth Cranberry Gingerbread with Brown Sugar Whipped Cream, page 201

Lemon Swirl Cheesecake, page 208

Flamed Orange Flan Cake, page 202

Baked Rhubarb, page 215

Steamed Persimmon Pudding, page 213

Big Lost River Strawberries, page 212

Champagne

Late Harvest Riesling

Whitewater Spicy Bean Cake

serves twelve

Ingredients

¼	cup butter, softened
2	eggs
2	cups mashed cooked pinto beans
1	cup flour
¼	teaspoon salt
1	teaspoon baking soda
1	cup sugar
1	teaspoon cinnamon
¼	teaspoon nutmeg
½	teaspoon ground cloves
2	cups chopped apples
¾	cup raisins
¼	cup chopped pecans
1½	teaspoons vanilla extract

This cake is delicious topped off with a maple-flavored frosting. If you prefer a chocolate cake, add ¼ cup of baking cocoa to the flour. It is compliments of the Idaho Bean Commission.

▲ Preheat the oven to 375 degrees and grease a 9x13-inch cake pan.

▲ Cream the butter in a mixer bowl and beat in the eggs one at a time. Blend in the beans.

▲ Sift the flour, salt, baking soda, sugar, cinnamon, nutmeg and cloves together. Add to the butter mixture, blending well. Fold in the apples, raisins, pecans and vanilla.

▲ Spoon into the cake pan. Bake for 45 to 50 minutes or until a wooden pick inserted into the center of the cake comes out clean. Cool on a wire rack.

Although native Americans and trappers could subsist on the local flora and fauna, it was not realistic for the emigrants to try to do so. They were too unfamiliar with wilderness living and there were too many people traveling the same route to make hunting and gathering the exclusive means of securing food. Not relying on the land meant that the overlanders had to transport their own kitchen and pantry.

WAGON WHEEL KITCHENS

Chocolate Rum Cake with Rum Sauce

serves twelve

Ingredients

1	(2-layer) package chocolate cake mix
1	(6-ounce) package chocolate instant pudding mix
½	cup vegetable oil
½	cup rum
½	cup water
4	eggs
1	cup chopped pecans
½	cup melted butter
1	cup sugar
½	cup rum

▲ Preheat the oven to 325 degrees and grease a bundt pan.

▲ Combine the cake mix, pudding mix, oil, rum, water and eggs in a large bowl and beat for 3 minutes. Fold in the pecans. Spoon into the bundt pan. Bake for 55 minutes. Cool in the pan for 15 minutes.

▲ Combine the melted butter, sugar and rum and beat until well blended. Pierce holes in the cake and pour the sauce over the top. Cool in the pan on a wire rack for 30 minutes. Remove to a serving plate.

Sheepherder's Chocolate Cake

serves twelve

Ingredients

1	(2-layer) package dark chocolate cake mix
⅓	cup packed brown sugar
4	eggs
1	cup sour cream
½	cup warm water
½	cup vegetable oil
6	ounces chocolate chips, melted
½	cup chocolate chips
2	tablespoons confectioners' sugar

▲ Preheat the oven to 350 degrees and grease and flour a bundt pan.

▲ Combine the cake mix, brown sugar, eggs, sour cream, water, oil and melted chocolate chips in a large bowl. Beat at medium speed for 4 minutes. Fold in the chocolate chips.

▲ Spoon into the bundt pan. Bake for 45 to 50 minutes or until a wooden pick inserted into the center of the cake comes out clean; do not overbake. Cool in the pan for 10 minutes and invert onto a wire rack to cool completely. Dust with confectioners' sugar.

Redfish Lake Chocolate Devil with Raspberry Sauce

serves twelve

Cake

16	ounces bittersweet or semi-sweet chocolate, chopped
10	tablespoons butter, softened
4	eggs
¼	cup sugar
1	tablespoon flour
1	cup chocolate curls

Whipped Cream Frosting

1	cup whipping cream
1	tablespoon confectioners' sugar
1	teaspoon vanilla extract

Raspberry Sauce

2	cups frozen raspberries, thawed
2 to 3	tablespoons sugar
1	tablespoon framboise or kirsch

▲ For the cake, preheat the oven to 425 degrees and butter an 8-inch round cake pan. Line the bottom with buttered parchment paper cut to fit. Flour the pan, tapping out excess flour. Melt the chocolate and butter in a double boiler over hot water.

▲ Combine the eggs and sugar in a metal bowl and place over the hot water. Cook until the sugar dissolves and the mixture is lukewarm, whisking constantly. Remove from the heat and beat for 5 to 10 minutes or until thickened and light. Fold in the flour. Fold ⅓ of the egg mixture into the chocolate. Fold in the remaining egg mixture gently.

▲ Spoon into the prepared cake pan. Bake for 15 minutes or until the center is soft and the top is crusty. Cool in the pan on a wire rack. Cover and freeze in the pan overnight.

▲ Remove the cake from the freezer early in the day. Dip the bottom of the pan in hot water to unmold the chocolate. Invert onto a flat serving plate and remove the parchment.

▲ For the frosting, whip the cream with the confectioners' sugar and vanilla in a bowl until it forms soft peaks. Chill until time to use. Spread ⅔ of the frosting on the cake and pipe the remaining frosting around the edge.

▲ For the sauce, purée the raspberries in a food processor and strain to remove the seeds. Stir in the sugar until dissolved and then add the liqueur and blend well. Chill until serving time.

▲ Spoon the sauce onto the serving plates and place thin wedges of the cake in the sauce. Garnish with chocolate curls.

Challis Chocolate Zucchini Cake
serves twelve

Ingredients

½	cup butter, softened
½	cup vegetable oil
1¾	cups sugar
2	eggs
1	teaspoon vanilla extract
½	cup sour cream or buttermilk
2	cups flour
¼	cup baking cocoa
½	teaspoon baking powder
1	teaspoon baking soda
½	teaspoon cinnamon
1	teaspoon ground cloves
2	cups grated zucchini
¼	cup chocolate chips
2	tablespoons confectioners' sugar

This cake can also be served with a cream cheese frosting or with your favorite ice cream.

▲ Preheat the oven to 325 degrees and grease and lightly flour a 9x13-inch cake pan.

▲ Cream the butter, oil and sugar in a mixer bowl until smooth. Add the eggs, vanilla and sour cream, blending well.

▲ Combine the flour, baking cocoa, baking powder, baking soda, cinnamon and cloves and add to the sugar mixture, mixing well. Fold in the zucchini and chocolate chips.

▲ Spoon into the cake pan. Bake for 40 to 45 minutes or until the cake springs back when lightly touched in the center. Cool in the pan for 10 minutes and invert onto a wire rack to cool completely. Dust with confectioners' sugar.

"My father and his contemporaries were the first permanent settlers. They built the first homes, established the first families. When he and my mother were married at Genesee on July 11, 1900, they had no house on Salmon River to go to. They lived in a dugout the first year, while he built a house of rough boards rafted from 25 miles upriver. Over the next 17 years, they lived in similar rough shacks and log cabins along the river and in the flanking mountains that provided summer range."

SALMON RIVER SAGA

Sawtooth Cranberry Gingerbread with Brown Sugar Whipped Cream

serves twelve

Gingerbread

3	cups flour
1½	teaspoons baking powder
1½	teaspoons cinnamon
1½	teaspoons ginger
¾	teaspoon baking soda
¾	teaspoon salt
¾	teaspoon allspice
¼	teaspoon ground cloves
¾	cup unsalted butter, softened
¾	cup packed dark brown sugar
2	eggs
1	cup plus 2 tablespoons unsulfured light molasses
1	cup plus 2 tablespoons buttermilk
2½	cups coarsely chopped cranberries
⅓	cup chopped crystallized ginger
	Cinnamon to taste

Brown Sugar Whipped Cream

1	cup whipping cream, chilled
⅓	cup sour cream, chilled
⅓	cup packed dark brown sugar
1½	teaspoons vanilla extract

▲ For the gingerbread, preheat the oven to 350 degrees and grease and flour a 9x13-inch cake pan.

▲ Sift the flour, baking powder, cinnamon, ginger, baking soda, salt, allspice and cloves into a medium bowl.

▲ Cream the butter in a mixer bowl until light. Add the brown sugar and beat until fluffy. Beat in the eggs one at a time. Mix in the molasses.

▲ Add the flour mixture and the buttermilk alternately to the sugar mixture, ending with the flour mixture and mixing well after each addition. Fold in the cranberries and crystallized ginger. Spoon into the cake pan.

▲ Bake for 50 minutes or until the cake springs back when lightly touched in the center. Cool in the pan on a wire rack.

▲ For the whipped cream, combine the whipping cream, sour cream, brown sugar and vanilla in a large mixer bowl. Beat until soft peaks form. Chill, covered, for up to 4 hours.

▲ Serve the cake warm or at room temperature with the whipped cream and a sprinkling of cinnamon.

Flamed Orange Flan Cake

serves six

Ingredients

1¾	cups sugar
¾	cup water
½	cup butter, softened
¼	cup flour
8	medium egg yolks, at room temperature, beaten
1	cup plus 2 tablespoons strained orange juice
8	medium egg whites, at room temperature
⅓	cup brandy

▲ Preheat the oven to 325 degrees.

▲ Combine ¾ cup sugar and the water in a heavy saucepan. Cook over medium heat until the mixture becomes a dark tan color, stirring constantly. Pour carefully and quickly into a 1½-quart baking dish.

▲ Cream the butter and ¾ cup sugar in a medium mixer bowl until smooth. Add the flour and mix well. Beat in the egg yolks and stir in the orange juice.

▲ Beat the egg whites in a mixer bowl until soft peaks form. Add ¼ cup sugar gradually, beating constantly until stiff peaks form. Fold into the butter mixture.

▲ Pour into the caramel-lined dish and set into a larger pan. Pour enough hot water into the larger pan to reach 1 inch up the side of the baking dish.

▲ Bake for 1 hour or until a knife inserted into the center comes out clean and the top is brown. Remove the baking dish from the pan of water immediately so the flan will not overcook. Cool on a wire rack and then refrigerate for 3 hours or longer. Run a knife around the edges of the flan to loosen and invert onto an ovenproof platter.

▲ Heat the brandy in a saucepan and pour over the flan. Ignite a small amount of the heated brandy in a long-handled spoon or ladle and use it to ignite the flan.

Chocolate Chip Cookies with Walnuts and Raisins

serves ninety-six

Ingredients

2	cups butter, softened
1½	cups packed brown sugar
½	cup sugar
2	large eggs
1	teaspoon vanilla extract
4	cups sifted flour
1	tablespoon baking soda
1	teaspoon salt
1	cup toasted chopped walnuts
1	cup raisins
12	ounces chocolate chips

▲ Preheat the oven to 375 degrees and grease the cookie sheets.

▲ Beat the butter, brown sugar, sugar, eggs and vanilla in a large mixer bowl for 3 minutes or until smooth. Combine the flour, baking soda and salt in a medium bowl and then add it to the butter mixture. Mix thoroughly and then stir in the walnuts, raisins and chocolate chips.

▲ Drop by heaping teaspoons 1½ inches apart onto the cookie sheets. Bake for 10 minutes or until golden brown. Cool for 1 minute before removing to a wire rack to cool completely. May wrap tightly and freeze if desired.

Float Trip Disappearing Chocolate Bars

serves nine

Ingredients

½	cup butterscotch chips
¼	cup butter
¾	cup flour
⅓	cup packed brown sugar
1	teaspoon baking powder
¼	teaspoon salt
1	egg
½	teaspoon vanilla extract
1	cup miniature marshmallows
1	cup semisweet chocolate chips
¼	cup chopped pecans

▲ Preheat the oven to 350 degrees and grease an 8x8-inch baking dish. Melt the butterscotch chips and butter in a medium saucepan over low heat, stirring constantly. Cool to lukewarm.

▲ Combine the flour, brown sugar, baking powder and salt in a small bowl and stir into the butterscotch mixture. Add the egg and vanilla, mixing well. Fold in the marshmallows, chocolate chips and pecans. Spoon into the baking dish.

▲ Bake for 20 to 25 minutes or until the center is still slightly soft; the center will firm up when cool. Cool on a wire rack. Cut into bars.

Desserts

Ranchers' Lemon Delights
serves seventy-four

Ingredients

½	cup margarine, softened
½	cup vegetable oil
½	cup sugar
½	cup confectioners' sugar
1	egg or ¼ cup egg substitute
	Several drops of lemon concentrate
2	cups plus 1 tablespoon flour
½	teaspoon baking powder
½	teaspoon cream of tartar
¼	teaspoon salt
½	teaspoon grated lemon rind
½	cup sugar

▲ Preheat the oven to 375 degrees.

▲ Combine the margarine, oil, ½ cup sugar and the confectioners' sugar in a large mixer bowl and beat until smooth. Add the egg and lemon concentrate, mixing well.

▲ Sift the flour, baking powder, cream of tartar, salt and lemon rind together. Blend into the sugar mixture.

▲ Place the remaining ½ cup sugar in a bowl. Shape the cookie dough into 1-inch balls and roll in the sugar to coat. Place 3 to 4 inches apart on ungreased cookie sheets. Dip the bottom of a drinking glass in additional sugar and press each cookie to flatten ⅛ inch thick.

▲ Bake until the edges begin to brown. Cool for 1 minute before removing cookies to wire racks to cool completely.

…that sometimes the meal on the trail was a simple one of 'plain middling meat, crackers and heavy biscuit.' Other times the meal was more varied: 'Had ham, dried beef, crackers, pickle and syrup for dinner with brandy today.' Crackers and hardtack were most appreciated on days when there was not enough time to bake bread, or if there was no fuel to start a fire…

George Curry and Ellen Tootle, 1846
WAGON WHEEL KITCHENS: FOOD ON THE OREGON TRAIL

White Chocolate Chip Cookies

serves forty-eight

Ingredients

1	cup butter, softened
1	cup sugar
1	cup packed brown sugar
2	eggs
1	teaspoon vanilla extract
2	tablespoons baking cocoa
½	teaspoon salt
1	teaspoon baking soda
1	teaspoon baking powder
2	cups flour
2½	cups quick-cooking oats
12	ounces white chocolate chips
1½	cups chopped almonds

▲ Preheat the oven to 350 degrees.

▲ Cream the butter, sugar and brown sugar in a food processor until smooth. Mix in the eggs and vanilla. Combine the cocoa, salt, baking soda and baking powder in a bowl. Add to the food processor and process until moistened.

▲ Mix in the flour, scraping down the side of the food processor container as needed. Pulse in the oats. Stir in the chocolate chips and almonds by hand.

▲ Shape into 2-inch balls. Place 2 inches apart on ungreased cookie sheets. Bake for 10 minutes. Remove to a wire rack to cool.

Apple-Blueberry Crispy Cobbler

serves six

Ingredients

1	pint fresh blueberries
2	cups sliced peeled tart apples
1	tablespoon lemon juice
½	cup packed brown sugar
1	cup flour
¾	cup sugar
1	teaspoon baking powder
¾	teaspoon salt
1	egg, lightly beaten
⅓	cup butter, melted, cooled
½	teaspoon cinnamon

▲ Preheat the oven to 350 degrees and butter an 8x8-inch baking dish.

▲ Combine the blueberries and apples in the baking dish. Sprinkle with the lemon juice and brown sugar.

▲ Combine the flour, sugar, baking powder and salt in a medium bowl. Add the egg and mix well. Sprinkle over the fruit and drizzle with the melted butter. Sprinkle with the cinnamon.

▲ Bake for 35 to 40 minutes or until the fruit is bubbling and the topping is brown. Serve warm with ice cream or whipped cream.

"Done some washing and I baked some bread and pumpkin and apple pies, cooked beans and meat, stewed apples and baked suckeyes in quantities sufficient to last some time…Besides making dutch cheese and took everything out of the wagons to air…"

Cecilia Adams, 1852, Covered Wagon Women: Diaries and Letters from the Western Trails
WOMEN'S VOICES FROM THE OREGON TRAIL

Almond Amaretto Cheesecake

serves sixteen

Crust

½	cup crushed Amaretto cookies
½	cup graham cracker crumbs
½	cup ground toasted almonds
¼	cup melted butter
1	tablespoon Amaretto

Cheesecake Filling

1	(8-ounce) can almond paste
½	cup sugar
2	tablespoons flour
⅓	cup Amaretto
24	ounces cream cheese, at room temperature, cubed
4	eggs

Topping

1	cup sour cream
2	tablespoons sugar
2	tablespoons Amaretto
1	cup whipped cream (optional)
½	cup toasted sliced almonds (optional)

▲ For the crust, combine the crushed cookies, graham cracker crumbs, toasted almonds, melted butter and Amaretto in a bowl and mix well.

▲ Press over the bottom and 1 inch up the side of a buttered 9-inch springform pan. Chill in the refrigerator.

▲ Preheat the oven to 350 degrees.

▲ For the filling, combine the almond paste, sugar and flour in a food processor fitted with a steel blade. Process until smooth. Add the Amaretto and the cream cheese 1 cube at a time, processing constantly until smooth. Add eggs one at a time, mixing well.

▲ Pour into the chilled pan. Bake for about 50 minutes or just until set; do not overbake. Increase the oven temperature to 400 degrees.

▲ For the topping, combine the sour cream, sugar and Amaretto in a bowl and mix well. Spread over the cheesecake and bake for 10 to 15 minutes longer. Cool in the pan on a wire rack. Chill until serving time.

▲ Place the pan on a serving plate and remove the side. Top with whipped cream and toasted almonds if desired.

Lemon Swirl Cheesecake

serves twelve

Crust

6	whole graham crackers
1	cup walnuts, toasted
3	tablespoons melted butter
2	teaspoons grated lemon rind

Cheesecake Filling

16	ounces cream cheese, softened
½	cup sugar
½	cup thawed frozen lemonade concentrate
2	teaspoons grated lemon rind
¾	cup sour cream, at room temperature
2	eggs
1	cup sour cream, at room temperature
1	(11-ounce) jar lemon curd
⅔	cup whipping cream, whipped
2	(¼-inch) lemon slices, each cut into 4 wedges
8	small mint sprigs

▲ Preheat the oven to 350 degrees and place a rack in the center of the oven.

▲ For the crust, process the graham crackers in a food processor until finely ground. Add the walnuts and process until coarsely chopped. Add the butter and lemon rind. Pulse to blend until the crumbs are just moistened.

▲ Press the crumbs firmly over the bottom of a 9-inch springform pan. Bake for 10 minutes or until set. Cool on a wire rack.

▲ For the filling, beat the cream cheese, sugar, lemonade concentrate and lemon rind in a large mixer bowl until smooth. Blend in ¾ cup sour cream and add the eggs one at a time, beating until just combined.

▲ Pour into the crust. Bake for 50 minutes or until the center of the cheesecake moves only slightly when the pan is shaken. Cool for 5 minutes on a wire rack.

▲ Whisk 1 cup sour cream in a small bowl until very smooth. Whisk the lemon curd in a small bowl until very smooth.

▲ Run a small knife around the edge of the cheesecake to loosen the side. Spoon small dollops of sour cream and lemon curd alternately on the warm cheesecake, starting at the outer edge, forming concentric circles and covering the cake completely. Shake the pan to smooth out the dollops and swirl with the tip of a knife to marbleize. Cover and chill for 8 hours.

▲ Pipe the whipped cream around the top edge of the cheesecake. Garnish with lemon slices and mint sprigs.

Individual Caramel Flans

serves twelve

Ingredients

1	cup sugar
1	tablespoon water
8	eggs
1½	cups sugar
½	teaspoon vanilla extract
½	teaspoon almond extract
½	teaspoon salt
1	quart milk, scalded

▲ Preheat the oven to 350 degrees.

▲ Sprinkle 1 cup sugar in a small heavy saucepan. Cook over medium-low heat for 7 to 10 minutes or until deep golden brown, stirring constantly. Add the water carefully and cook for 1 minute, stirring constantly. Pour into 12 small custard cups, tilting to coat the sides.

▲ Beat the eggs lightly in a large bowl. Add 1½ cups sugar, flavorings and salt, mixing well. Stir in the milk gradually.

▲ Pour into the custard cups. Place the cups in a large pan and pour in enough hot water to reach 1 inch up the sides of the cups. Bake for 30 minutes or until a knife inserted in the center comes out clean.

▲ Let cool and chill overnight in the refrigerator. Run a knife around each flan and invert onto individual dishes.

Sherried Cream with Red Grapes

serves four

Ingredients

⅓	cup sugar
2	tablespoons cornstarch
⅛	teaspoon salt
2	cups milk
¼	cup cream sherry or apple juice
2	egg yolks, lightly beaten
2	tablespoons butter
1	teaspoon vanilla extract
1½	cups seedless red grapes

This is a nice light dessert to follow a hearty meal.

▲ Mix the sugar, cornstarch and salt in a 2-quart saucepan. Add the milk and sherry gradually, stirring until well blended.

▲ Bring to a boil over medium heat, stirring constantly. Boil for 1 minute and remove from the heat.

▲ Stir a small amount of the hot mixture into the beaten egg yolks; stir the egg yolks into the hot mixture. Cook for 30 seconds longer. Remove from the heat and stir in the butter and vanilla. Alternate layers of pudding and grapes in 4 stemmed glasses. Chill and serve.

Crème Anglaise

serves two

Ingredients

1	cup milk
¾	cup cream
½	cup sugar
4	egg yolks, beaten
1	teaspoon cornstarch
	Salt to taste
1	teaspoon vanilla extract
1	cup whipped cream (optional)

Serve this creamy custard, warm or chilled, over ripe pear or peach halves.

▲ Heat the milk and cream in a double boiler. Combine the sugar, egg yolks, cornstarch and salt in a bowl and stir into the hot milk. Cook over hot water for 7 minutes or until it will coat the back of a spoon, stirring constantly. Cool to room temperature. Fold in the vanilla and whipped cream.

▲ Pour into a bowl or a serving pitcher and chill until serving time.

Lime Fool with Strawberries and Kiwifruit

serves four

Ingredients

¼	cup whipping cream
¼	cup fresh lime juice
1	teaspoon grated lime rind
6	ounces imported white chocolate, chopped
¾	cup whipping cream
3	tablespoons sugar
2	cups sliced strawberries
2	kiwifruit, peeled, thinly sliced
4	whole strawberries
4	lime slices

▲ Bring ¼ cup whipping cream, lime juice and lime rind to a simmer in a small heavy saucepan. Reduce the heat to low and add the chocolate. Cook until melted and smooth, stirring constantly. Pour into a medium bowl and chill for 25 minutes or until cool but not set.

▲ Beat the remaining ¾ cup whipping cream in a medium mixer bowl until thickened. Add the sugar and beat until soft peaks form. Fold into the chilled chocolate mixture.

▲ Place a scant ¼ cup of the strawberries in each of four 8- to 10-ounce wine glasses. Press 3 kiwifruit slices against the side of each glass. Spoon ⅓ cup of the chocolate mixture into each glass. Spoon a scant ¼ cup of strawberries into the center of each, pressing so that the strawberries are not visible through the sides of the glasses. Spoon the remaining chocolate mixture on top and smooth the surface. Cover and chill for 2 to 6 hours.

▲ Slice the whole strawberries, cutting to but not through the stem end. Fan out on top of each serving. Place 1 lime slice on the rim of each glass.

STRAWBERRY DUMPLINGS: Wet up some light dough roll it up with a bottle. Spread the berries over it and roll up in a cloth and boil it. Make a cup full of sauce with the juice of the berries and a little sugar and nutmeg. Serve the sauce over the dumplings...

Mary Powers, 1856, Women's Travails and Triumphs on the Overland Trails
WOMEN'S VOICES FROM THE OREGON TRAIL

Big Lost River Strawberries

serves six

Ingredients

¾ cup sugar
½ cup heavy cream
¼ cup light corn syrup
2 tablespoons butter
½ cup chopped toffee candy bars
1 quart fresh strawberries
1 cup sour cream

This is an impressive dessert that is so good and so easy.

▲ Combine the sugar, cream, corn syrup and butter in a small saucepan. Bring to a boil and cook for 3 minutes, stirring occasionally to prevent boiling over. Remove from the heat and stir in the chopped candy until most of the candy is dissolved. Cool to room temperature.

▲ Place the strawberries in individual serving dishes, top with a dollop of sour cream and drizzle with the toffee sauce. Serve immediately.

Fresh Fruit with Sabayon Gratin

serves six

Ingredients

6 egg yolks
⅓ cup sugar
⅔ cup sauterne or late-harvest riesling
3 cups fresh berries
3 cups fresh peaches
Sections of 3 navel oranges

▲ Preheat the broiler.

▲ Combine the egg yolks, sugar and wine in a large round stainless steel bowl. Place the bowl over a pan of simmering water and whisk until light and frothy. Cook for 10 minutes longer or until the mixture is thickened and quadrupled in volume, stirring constantly. Set over a bowl of ice and stir to cool quickly.

▲ Layer the berries, peaches and oranges in a gratin dish or individual baking dishes. Top with the sabayon, allowing some fruit to show. Broil 4 inches from the heat source for 15 to 20 seconds or until the sabayon is glazed and slightly browned. Serve immediately.

Steamed Persimmon Pudding

serves four

Ingredients

½ cup melted butter
1 cup sugar
1 cup sifted flour
¼ teaspoon salt
1 teaspoon cinnamon
2 teaspoons baking soda
2 teaspoons warm water
3 tablespoons brandy or bourbon
1 teaspoon vanilla extract
1 cup very ripe persimmon pulp
2 eggs, slightly beaten
1 cup seedless raisins
½ cup chopped walnuts

Sprinkle this pudding with brandy and flame it for a special touch. Serve it with hard sauce.

▲ Blend the butter and sugar in a bowl. Sift in the flour, salt and cinnamon and mix well.

▲ Dissolve the baking soda in the water, brandy and vanilla in a medium bowl. Stir in the persimmon pulp. Add to the butter mixture, mixing well. Add the eggs, mixing lightly. Stir in the raisins and walnuts.

▲ Pour into a buttered pudding mold. Cover tightly with foil and lid and place on a rack in a steamer over a small amount of water; the pan should not touch the water. Steam for 2½ to 3 hours, adding more hot water as needed.

▲ Cool on a rack for 15 minutes and unmold onto a serving plate. Wrap and store in the refrigerator or freezer until serving time.

Salmon River Chocolate Pecan Pudding with Bourbon Sauce
serves eight

Pudding

4	ounces semisweet chocolate, chopped
3	tablespoons hot water
⅓	cup sugar
1	cup chopped pecans
¼	cup dry bread crumbs
¼	teaspoon cinnamon
½	cup unsalted butter, softened
1½	tablespoons bourbon
5	egg yolks
5	egg whites
	Salt to taste

Bourbon Sauce

1½	cups milk
⅓	cup sugar
4	egg yolks
2½	tablespoons bourbon
1½	teaspoons vanilla extract

▲ Preheat the oven to 350 degrees and butter an 8x8-inch baking dish or 1½-quart baking dish.

▲ For the pudding, melt the chocolate in the hot water in a bowl, whisking until smooth. Cool to room temperature.

▲ Process 1 tablespoon of the sugar with ½ cup of the pecans in a food processor until finely ground. Add the bread crumbs and cinnamon and pulse to blend. Set aside.

▲ Cream the butter with half the remaining sugar in a large mixer bowl until light. Beat in the cooled chocolate and then the bourbon. Beat in the egg yolks 1 at a time. Stir in the ground pecan mixture.

▲ Beat the egg whites with the salt until very soft peaks form. Add the remaining sugar gradually, beating constantly until soft peaks form. Fold in the egg whites gradually.

▲ Pour into the baking dish and smooth the top; sprinkle with the remaining chopped pecans. Place the baking dish in a larger pan and add enough hot water to reach halfway up the side. Bake for 30 to 35 minutes or until puffed and slightly firm. Do not overbake.

▲ For the sauce, combine the milk and sugar in a medium nonreactive saucepan. Bring to a boil over moderate heat. Beat the egg yolks in a small bowl. Whisk in ⅓ of the hot milk. Return the remaining milk to low heat and add the yolk mixture, stirring constantly. Cook for 1 to 1½ minutes or until thickened; do not boil. Remove from the heat. Whisk constantly for 1 minute to cool. Strain through a sieve and whisk for 30 seconds longer. Stir in the bourbon and vanilla. Serve warm over the pudding.

Baked Rhubarb

serves six

Ingredients

3	cups (about) 1-inch rhubarb pieces
3	cups cubed soft bread
½	cup sugar
½	cup packed brown sugar
½	cup melted butter

This is a surprising and absolutely delicious dessert. It's also great with ice cream and freezes well.

▲ Preheat the oven to 350 degrees and grease a 2-quart baking dish.

▲ Combine the rhubarb, bread cubes, sugar, brown sugar and butter in a large bowl and mix well. Pour into the baking dish and bake for 1 hour. Serve warm.

Frozen Chocolate Pecan Pie

serves eight

Pecan Pie Shell

2	cups finely chopped pecans, toasted
5	tablespoons plus 1 teaspoon packed brown sugar
¼	cup butter, chilled, cut into small pieces
2	teaspoons dark rum

Filling

6	ounces semisweet chocolate
½	teaspoon instant coffee
4	eggs, at room temperature
1	tablespoon dark rum
1	teaspoon vanilla extract
1½	cups whipping cream
3	tablespoons shaved semisweet chocolate

▲ For the pie shell, mix the pecans, brown sugar, butter and rum in a bowl and mix well. Press over the bottom and side of a 9-inch pie plate. Freeze for 1 hour or longer.

▲ For the filling, melt the chocolate with the coffee granules in a double boiler over hot water. Remove from the heat and cool slightly.

▲ Whisk in the eggs, rum and vanilla until smooth. Cool for about 5 minutes. Pour into the pie shell. Freeze until firm.

▲ Beat the whipping cream in a mixer bowl until soft peaks form. Spoon over the frozen pie. Garnish with shaved chocolate.

Eggnog Chiffon Pie

serves eight

Ingredients

1	tablespoon unflavored gelatin
1¾	cups eggnog
3	egg yolks
¼	cup sugar
3	egg whites
¼	cup sugar
½	teaspoon vanilla extract
1	cup whipping cream, whipped
1	baked (9-inch) pie shell

▲ Soften the gelatin in ¼ cup of the eggnog and set aside.

▲ Heat the remaining eggnog in a saucepan until hot but not boiling. Beat the egg yolks lightly in a small bowl and stir in ¼ cup sugar. Stir a small amount of the hot eggnog into the egg yolks; stir the egg yolks into the hot eggnog. Cook over medium heat until the mixture coats the back of a spoon, stirring constantly. Remove from the heat and stir in the gelatin until dissolved. Cool to room temperature.

▲ Beat the egg whites in a medium bowl until foamy. Add ¼ cup sugar and beat until stiff peaks form. Fold the egg whites, vanilla, and half of the whipped cream into the chilled eggnog mixture.

▲ Spoon into the pie shell and top with the remaining whipped cream.

"Louis was only a small boy when the family moved…He told of the pack train which moved them, saying that the pots and pans, and buckets, rattled all the way. Bacon was brought in by the pack trains in slabs, and sold that way. It would keep fairly well during the summer, but if kept very long it developed a 'rusty' appearance. It not only supplied meat, but every drop of 'grease' was used in one way or another…it was even used to make fruit pies—it added a special flavor to the crust."

FOOTPRINTS ON MOUNTAIN TRAILS

Cream Cheese Banana Pie

serves eight

Ingredients

3	medium bananas, sliced
1	baked (9-inch) pie shell
8	ounces cream cheese, softened
1	(14-ounce) can sweetened condensed milk
⅓	cup fresh lemon juice
1	teaspoon vanilla extract
8	mint leaves
4	thin lemon slices

▲ Arrange the banana slices in the pie shell, overlapping as necessary.

▲ Beat the cream cheese in a mixer bowl until light and fluffy. Beat in the condensed milk gradually. Add the lemon juice and vanilla, mixing well.

▲ Pour into the prepared pie shell and chill for 2 hours. Top with pairs of mint leaves and twisted lemon slices.

Huckleberry Cream Cheese Pie

serves eight

Ingredients

8	ounces cream cheese, softened
¼	cup sour cream
½	teaspoon vanilla extract
¼	cup sugar
1	baked (9-inch) pie shell, cooled
3	cups fresh huckleberries
½	cup water
½	cup sugar
2	tablespoons cornstarch
1	tablespoon fresh lemon juice

▲ Blend the cream cheese, sour cream, vanilla and ¼ cup sugar in a medium bowl until smooth. Spread evenly in the pie shell and chill until firm.

▲ Mash 1 cup of the huckleberries in a small saucepan and add the water. Bring to a boil and strain through a sieve. Add enough water to the berry juice to make 1 cup of liquid.

▲ Combine ½ cup sugar with the cornstarch in a bowl. Combine with the strained liquid in a saucepan. Cook until thickened and bubbly, stirring constantly. Remove from the heat and stir in the lemon juice. Cool.

▲ Arrange the remaining 2 cups of the huckleberries over the cream cheese layer. Spoon the huckleberry glaze over the berries. Chill for 3 hours.

PUMPKIN SUNDAE PIE

serves eight

Pie

1¼	cups sugar
1	cup canned pumpkin
1	teaspoon pumpkin pie spice
½	teaspoon salt
1	cup whipping cream, whipped
2	pints vanilla ice cream, softened
1	baked (9-inch) pie shell

Caramel Sauce

1	cup packed brown sugar
½	cup light corn syrup
½	cup water
1	teaspoon vanilla extract

▲ For the pie, combine the sugar, pumpkin, pumpkin pie spice and salt in a large bowl. Fold in the whipped cream gradually.

▲ Spoon 1½ pints of the ice cream into the pie shell. Top with the pumpkin mixture, swirling with a spoon to marbleize. Spoon the remaining ice cream in a circle around the edge. Freeze for 2 hours or longer.

▲ For the caramel sauce, blend the brown sugar, corn syrup and water in a small saucepan. Bring to a boil over medium heat and cook for 5 minutes. Remove from the heat and stir in the vanilla.

▲ Drizzle some of the warm caramel sauce on the pie. Serve with the remaining sauce.

"We three had been invited to dinner with different bachelors. In this way I was able to observe the method of their house cleaning, cooking and hospitality. The main company meal usually consisted of beans, biscuits, bacon, and sometimes fried eggs, syrup and honey. One homesteader decided to make a custard pie. He put baking powder in the crust, which raised up so much that most of the filling went over the edge and into the oven."

SALMON RIVER SAGA

Puffed Apple Tarts

serves eight

Ingredients

8	small tart apples, peeled, sliced
¼	cup sugar
1	teaspoon vanilla extract
3	tablespoons butter
¼	cup apricot jam
1	pound frozen puff pastry, thawed
1	tablespoon butter, chopped
1	egg, beaten

▲ Preheat the oven to 400 degrees. Reserve 8 slices of apple.

▲ Combine the remaining apples with the sugar, vanilla and 3 tablespoons butter in a saucepan. Cover and cook for 5 minutes or until tender. Cool to room temperature and mash.

▲ Melt the apricot jam in a small saucepan and cool.

▲ Place the puff pastry on a work surface. Cut into sixteen 4-inch rounds. Place half the rounds on an ungreased baking sheet and prick all over with a fork. Brush with the melted jam.

▲ Spread the apple mixture to within ½ inch of the edges. Place an apple slice on top of each round and add a dot of butter. Brush the edges with the beaten egg.

▲ Roll the remaining 8 rounds about ½ inch wider than the first 8 rounds. Place on top of the filled rounds. Seal the edges with a fork. Brush with the beaten egg and make a small slit in the tops.

▲ Bake for 30 minutes or until brown. Serve warm with vanilla ice cream.

Custard Tart with Sautéed Pears

serves ten

Pastry

1½	cups flour
1	tablespoon sugar
½	cup butter, chopped
⅔	cup ice water

Filling

4	firm Anjou pears, peeled
2	tablespoons butter
2	tablespoons packed brown sugar

Custard

2	eggs
⅓	cup sugar
⅓	cup reserved pear sauté liquid
⅓	cup flour
½	teaspoon vanilla extract
1	cup heavy cream
3 to 4	tablespoons fruit liqueur (optional)

This is a favorite recipe of the Boise Art Museum Director, Dennis O'Leary. It's a guaranteed hit at a party.

▲ For the pastry, combine the flour, sugar, and butter in a bowl or food processor and process until crumbly. Add the ice water gradually, processing just until the mixture forms a slightly dry dough. Roll into a long strip on a lightly floured surface. Fold into thirds, turn 1 quarter turn and roll again into a long strip. Fold in thirds again and chill for 1 hour. Repeat the rolling process and shape into a ball. Chill for 1 hour.

▲ Preheat the oven to 400 degrees. Roll the pastry into a large circle and fit into an 11-inch fluted tart pan with a removable bottom, shaping up and over the rim of the pan. Line with foil and weight with pie weights. Bake for 15 minutes. Remove the pie weights and foil and bake for 7 to 10 minutes longer or until the crust begins to turn golden. Cool on a wire rack.

▲ For the filling, cut the pears into halves and discard the cores. Cut the halves into 24 slices. Heat the butter in a nonstick skillet. Add the brown sugar and stir until smooth. Add the pear slices in batches and sauté just until tender, adding more butter and brown sugar if necessary; remove the pears and cooking juices to a bowl.

▲ For the custard, beat the eggs and sugar in a medium bowl until thick and lemon-colored. Drain the pears, reserving ⅓ cup of the sauté liquid. Add to the eggs with the flour, vanilla, cream and liqueur. Beat until the mixture just begins to thicken.

▲ Pour into the prepared tart shell, filling halfway. Arrange the pear slices cut side down in the custard, starting with 4 slices in the center to form a cross. Arrange the remaining slices to radiate outward from the center in a decorative design. Bake in the center of the oven for 20 to 25 minutes or until the custard is set and golden. Cool before serving.

Raspberry Truffle Tart

serves ten

Raspberry Coulis

1	(12-ounce) package frozen raspberries or 1 to 1½ pints fresh raspberries
½	cup sugar

Pastry

6	tablespoons unsalted butter, softened
½	cup sugar
¾	cup flour
⅓	cup baking cocoa
½	teaspoon vanilla extract
⅛	teaspoon salt

Filling

10	ounces semisweet chocolate
5	tablespoons raspberry liqueur
1¼	cups heavy cream, at room temperature
1	cup whipped cream
10	raspberries
20	small mint leaves

This recipe is so rich with chocolate, it will keep you awake if you eat it right before bedtime! Marilyn Slaby won a National Dessert Contest with it on the Mike and Maty Television Show.

▲ For the coulis, press the raspberries through a sieve or food mill to remove the seeds. Combine with the sugar in a bowl and mix well. Chill until serving time.

▲ Preheat the oven to 350 degrees. Grease an 11-inch fluted tart pan with a removable bottom.

▲ For the pastry, cream the butter and sugar in a medium mixer bowl until light and fluffy. Blend in the flour, cocoa, vanilla and salt at a low speed to form a soft dough.

▲ Press over the bottom and side of the prepared pan. Bake for 8 to 10 minutes or until firm but not crisp; cool. Remove the side of the pan and place the tart shell on a serving platter.

▲ For the filling, place the chocolate in a medium glass bowl and pour the raspberry liqueur over the top. Microwave on High for 2 minutes or until nearly melted, whisking until smooth. Microwave for 45 seconds longer if necessary.

▲ Whisk in the heavy cream until smooth and blended. Pour into the tart shell and cool at room temperature for 2 hours. Store in the refrigerator or freezer.

▲ Cut the tart into wedges and serve on plates napped with the coulis. Garnish with whipped cream, raspberries and mint leaves.

Gallery Nine

Après Idaho

From Payette Lake to Hell's Canyon and from the Sawtooths to the Snake River Canyon, Idaho remains a mystery to most and a revelation to those few who stumble on her secrets. The roadless acres of wilderness seem to make the mystique grow and serve as a beacon to hardy souls. White collars and cowboys, sheepherders and river guides, skiers and movie stars all are part of Idaho's spirit. If you come, explore. If you're here, open your eyes to all that's around you. If you leave, take with you the secrets. If you have this book, think of it as the beginning, not the end.

"A lot of state, this Idaho, that I didn't know about"…
—Ernest Hemingway, 1939

Nutritional Profile Guidelines

The editors have attempted to present these family recipes in a form that allows approximate nutritional values to be computed. Persons with dietary or health problems or whose diets require close monitoring should not rely solely on the nutritional information provided. They should consult their physicians or a registered dietitian for specific information.

Abbreviations for Nutritional Profile

Cal — Calories	Fiber — Dietary Fiber	Sod — Sodium
Prot — Protein	T Fat — Total Fat	g — Grams
Carbo — Carbohydrates	Chol — Cholesterol	mg — Milligrams

Nutritional information for these recipes is computed from information derived from many sources, including materials supplied by the United States Department of Agriculture, computer databanks and journals in which the information is assumed to be in the public domain. However, many specialty items, new products and processed foods may not be available from these sources or may vary from the average values used in these profiles. More information on new and/or specific products may be obtained by reading the nutrient labels. Unless otherwise specified, the nutritional profile of these recipes is based on all measurements being level. If a choice of ingredients has been given, the nutritional profile reflects the first option. If a choice of amounts has been given, the nutritional profile reflects the greater amount.

Artificial sweeteners vary in use and strength so should be used "to taste," using the recipe ingredients as a guideline. Sweeteners using aspartame (NutraSweet and Equal) should not be used as a sweetener in recipes involving prolonged heating which reduces the sweet taste. For further information on the use of these sweeteners, refer to package information.

Alcoholic ingredients have been analyzed for basic ingredients, although cooking causes the evaporation of alcohol, thus decreasing caloric content.

Buttermilk, sour cream and *yogurt* are the types available commercially.

Cake mixes which are prepared using package directions include 3 eggs and 1/2 cup oil.

Chicken, cooked for boning and chopping, has been roasted; this method yields the lowest caloric values.

Cottage cheese is cream-style with 4.2% creaming mixture. Dry curd cottage cheese has no creaming mixture.

Eggs are all large. To avoid raw eggs that may carry salmonella in such recipes as eggnog or 6-week muffin batter, use an equivalent amount of commercial egg substitute.

Flour is unsifted all-purpose flour.

Garnishes, serving suggestions and other optional additions and variations are not included in the profile.

Margarine and *butter* are regular, not whipped or presoftened.

Milk is whole milk, 3.5% butterfat. Low-fat milk is 1% butterfat. Evaporated milk is whole milk with 60% of the water removed.

Oil is any type of vegetable cooking oil. *Shortening* is hydrogenated vegetable shortening.

Salt and other ingredients "to taste" as noted in the ingredients have not been included in the nutritional profile.

Page No.	Recipe Title	No. Servings	Cal	Prot (g)	Carbo (g)	T Fat (g)	% Cal From Fat	Chol (mg)	Fiber (g)	Sod (mg)
11	Bruschetta	8	201	4	21	12	52	1	2	154
12	Marinated Green Beans*	12	60	2	8	3	43	0	2	348
13	Cheese Capers	48	56	2	3	4	61	7	<1	101
14	Chicken Bites with Apricot Ginger Sauce	8	154	14	11	6	36	44	1	192
15	Chicken Wings with Garlic and Honey	18	194	16	8	11	52	48	<1	228
16	Stuffed Mushrooms	36	30	1	1	3	74	12	<1	30
17	Star Garnet Gougere Wreath	8	278	13	13	19	62	157	<1	394
18	Schweitzer Lamb Cocktail Meatballs	15	144	12	2	9	59	58	<1	415
19	Mine Shaft Beef Satay	8	358	32	7	22	56	89	1	1098
20	Chicken and Shrimp Satay with Peanut Sauce	8	394	36	21	20	44	82	2	2265
21	Pend Oreille Pot Stickers	8	318	12	21	20	58	31	<1	405
22	Silver Valley Dilled Shrimp	10	354	15	8	30	74	151	<1	394
22	Marinated Shrimp with Capers and Lemon*	20	307	18	7	24	68	159	<1	613
23	Bonner's Ferry Smoked Turkey in Pumpkin Biscuits	26	121	7	13	5	36	16	1	181
24	Cheese and Garlic-Stuffed Tomatoes	24	36	1	1	3	81	10	<1	29
24	Cedar Street Tortilla Roll-Ups	50	50	4	6	1	25	6	<1	233
25	Priest Lake Vegetable Wraps	10	158	4	21	7	39	1	3	298
26	Turkey Wrap-arounds	16	120	6	6	8	58	18	1	131
26	Beef Wrap-arounds	16	123	7	6	8	59	22	<1	117
27	Cataldo Mission Vegetarian Pizza Delight	15	116	2	6	10	73	20	1	236
28	Round Lake Zucchini and Rice Strudels	12	110	3	13	5	43	17	1	103
29	Black Bean Salsa with Cilantro and Lime	30	41	2	7	1	14	0	2	125
30	Post Falls Smoked Salmon Spread	8	152	6	1	14	81	68	<1	258
30	Kokanee Smoked Trout Mousse	15	133	6	1	12	80	41	<1	220
31	Thyme and Garlic Spread	16	106	2	2	10	83	31	<1	206
31	Cream Cheese Spread with Sun-Dried Tomatoes and Basil	16	104	1	2	10	87	30	<1	105
32	Creamy Almond and Crab Dip	8	134	6	2	12	77	46	<1	174
33	Hot Artichoke Dip with Parmesan Cheese	12	181	4	3	17	84	17	<1	478

Page No.	Recipe Title	No. Servings	Cal	Prot (g)	Carbo (g)	T Fat (g)	% Cal From Fat	Chol (mg)	Fiber (g)	Sod (mg)
							Approximate Per Serving			
33	Emerald Creek Bleu Cheese Dip	6	157	3	2	16	88	21	<1	237
34	Kootenai Cheese Dip	20	327	10	4	30	82	59	<1	850
34	Coeur D'Alene Caviar	16	49	1	3	4	71	0	1	328
35	Cucumber Dip	10	95	2	2	9	90	26	<1	689
35	Dilled Crackers	12	225	2	20	15	60	0	1	534
36	Glazed Almonds	32	263	8	20	19	60	0	4	144
37	Silver Mountain Margaritas	12	97	<1	12	<1	<1	0	<1	1
37	Cranberry Margaritas	6	241	<1	38	<1	1	0	1	4
38	Fourth of July Pass Caffé Latté Punch	16	116	1	11	7	55	28	<1	20
38	Lookout Pass Fruit Punch	50	81	1	20	<1	1	0	<1	8
39	Spiced Cranberry Punch	16	151	<1	39	<1	1	0	<1	3
39	Champagne Punch	24	110	<1	4	0	0	0	0	6
43	Lewis and Clark Argula and Orange Salad	4	290	14	18	19	57	22	5	702
44	Elk Creek Asparagus and Prosciutto Salad	6	149	9	6	11	61	27	2	384
45	Bitterroot Herbed Bean Salad	6	248	10	32	10	35	0	9	289
46	Lolo Pass Coleslaw	8	137	6	14	8	48	0	4	237
47	Red Cabbage Salad with Bacon and Goat Cheese	6	515	16	6	48	83	56	2	511
48	Minted Cucumber Salad	8	75	2	7	5	52	4	2	551
48	Fresh Mushroom Salad	6	269	5	7	26	84	5	2	108
49	Couscous Provençal	6	162	4	25	6	30	0	2	321
50	Warm Roasted Eggplant Salad with Bell Peppers and Tomatoes	8	131	2	12	10	61	0	5	10
51	Goose Creek Pear and Bleu Cheese Salad	8	228	4	15	19	69	4	2	166
52	Port and Stilton Salad	12	251	6	4	24	84	21	1	425
53	Spinach Salad with Chèvre and Roasted Shallots	4	1211	36	38	107	77	89	7	443
54	Sacajawea Tomato and Green Bean Salad	8	183	2	8	17	79	0	2	11
54	Clearwater Hot Chicken Salad	12	484	19	9	42	77	73	2	563
55	Hells Canyon Chicken Salad	8	394	29	18	23	53	72	2	1104
56	Cottonwood Butte Chicken Caesar Salad	8	379	19	7	31	74	66	2	343

Page No.	Recipe Title	No. Servings	Cal	Prot (g)	Carbo (g)	T Fat (g)	% Cal From Fat	Chol (mg)	Fiber (g)	Sod (mg)
							Approximate Per Serving			
57	Curried Chicken Salad with Chutney and Grapes	6	488	31	19	33	60	101	2	784
58	Palouse Chicken Salad	8	278	27	25	8	26	69	2	257
59	Whitewater Chicken and Pasta Salad	8	526	17	52	30	49	18	5	862
60	China Creek Pork Salad	4	445	41	23	21	42	110	6	2202
61	River Rafters' Shrimp Summer Salad Platter	8	220	25	5	11	46	221	2	519
62	Shrimp and Pasta Salad with Oranges	4	610	26	63	29	42	158	8	604
63	Round-Up Summer Bread and Pasta Salad	6	506	12	70	21	36	1	6	175
67	Idaho City Chicken and Bean Soup	4	409	46	24	14	31	95	8	2052
68	Payette River Chicken Bisque	4	977	65	39	62	57	306	6	6577
69	German Goulash Soup	12	306	24	25	13	37	71	4	373
70	Garden Valley Chilled Pea Soup	8	144	4	7	12	71	41	2	408
71	Ponderosa Tortilla Soup	4	406	17	46	19	41	22	6	2567
72	Roasted Tomato Soup with Spinach Pesto	4	888	27	28	81	76	76	8	1016
73	Packer John's Wild Game Potage	12	301	27	10	12	37	64	2	752
74	Hill House Cinnamon Rolls	18	295	4	31	18	54	67	<1	112
75	Sunshine Berry Coffee Cake	12	465	5	53	27	51	93	2	316
76	Warm Lake Coffee Cakes	16	339	7	56	10	26	39	2	322
77	Winter Carnival Walnut-Topped Brunch Cake	10	483	6	49	30	55	102	1	304
78	Horseshoe Bend Angel Biscuits	24	194	4	22	10	46	3	1	247
78	Brundage Sweet Corn Bread	12	369	6	51	16	39	109	1	319
79	Turn-of-the-Century Waffles	4	517	15	55	26	46	163	2	679
80	Cascade Banana Bread	8	220	5	47	2	7	54	1	219
81	Long Valley Oatmeal Carrot Bread	8	435	10	77	11	21	8	4	338
82	Payette Lake Baguettes	8	302	9	62	1	4	27	2	543
83	Mrs. Hofstetter's Potato Bread	36	280	8	59	1	6	0	3	536
84	Featherville Quick Loaf Bread	12	290	8	69	2	6	0	3	357
85	Whitewater Kranz	9	418	8	68	13	28	72	2	120
89	Baked Vegetables Provençal	4	204	2	18	15	62	0	7	70

Page No.	Recipe Title	No. Servings	Cal	Prot (g)	Carbo (g)	T Fat (g)	% Cal From Fat	Chol (mg)	Fiber (g)	Sod (mg)
							Approximate Per Serving			
90	Green Beans with Balsamic-Glazed Onions	10	173	4	18	11	53	6	6	264
91	Green Beans Caesar	8	69	2	10	3	4	8	4	448
91	Sautéed Green Beans with Radishes	8	50	1	5	3	53	4	2	89
92	Broccoli with Pine Nuts and Raisins	6	213	6	19	15	58	0	4	24
93	Warm Springs Carrots and Grapes	6	137	2	33	<1	3	0	4	41
93	Sautéed Carrots	8	122	1	7	10	74	0	2	39
94	Jordan Valley Jalapeño Corn Casserole	9	406	11	24	31	66	129	2	568
95	Gold Rush Burgundy Mushrooms	16	226	3	7	18	68	47	1	366
95	Spicy Glazed Onions	8	165	2	13	9	47	23	2	95
96	Braised Peas with Lettuce	8	217	7	22	12	49	31	6	402
96	Minted Peas in Tomato Cups	8	108	4	14	5	39	12	4	119
97	Tomatoes with Balsamic Vinegar and Povolone	4	302	16	12	22	64	39	2	512
97	Bugus Basin Broiled Tomatoes with Sherry	8	137	2	5	12	77	11	1	279
98	Breakfast Soufflé	6	830	35	48	55	60	567	3	1272
98	Eggs Fantastic	6	603	38	7	48	71	342	1	1379
99	Birds of Prey Fruit Compote	12	348	2	85	1	3	0	4	65
99	Cranberry Sauce with Mint Garnish	10	94	<1	24	<1	3	0	2	48
100	Hull's Gulch Potatoes Boulangerie	4	298	4	44	12	36	23	4	99
100	Boise River Festival Potato Strata	8	546	13	40	38	62	87	3	682
101	Owyhees Crab-Stuffed Potatoes	8	331	11	21	24	63	91	1	573
102	Christmas Potatoes	8	229	5	35	8	31	24	3	432
103	Sage and Garlic Mashed Potatoes	8	212	3	26	11	46	8	2	20
104	Peregrine Potato Gratin with Thyme	10	181	2	24	9	42	0	2	142
105	Shafer Butte Barley Pilaf	8	319	6	43	12	34	31	9	320
106	Idaho City Fiesta Fice	12	217	6	39	5	19	0	3	757
107	Lucky Peak Jasmine Rice	6	329	13	32	16	45	188	1	255
108	Boise River Rice and Pineapple	10	316	8	49	10	28	25	1	1048
109	Silver City Wild Rice	6	410	16	38	23	49	75	1	1130

Page No.	Recipe Title	No. Servings	Cal	Prot (g)	Carbo (g)	T Fat (g)	% Cal From Fat	Chol (mg)	Fiber (g)	Sod (mg)
							Approximate Per Serving			
110	Roasted Garlic and Wild Rice Mushroom Risotto	6	380	13	50	13	31	7	3	606
111	Athenian Orzo	4	255	10	32	9	32	27	4	1015
112	Pasta and Artichokes in Garlic Cream Sauce	8	346	11	47	13	34	30	3	565
113	Snake River Canyon Mushroom Pasta	4	355	11	55	9	21	0	5	24
114	Pasta with Spinach and Almonds	4	316	14	55	6	15	4	6	1794
115	Falcon Spinach Lasagna	8	615	37	35	38	54	104	6	698
119	Beef and Asparagus Rolls with Bleu Cheese Sauce	4	589	50	7	38	59	180	1	1305
120	Beef with Broccoli in Oyster Sauce	4	507	28	38	28	49	59	4	343
121	Bruneau Dunes Stuffed Flank Steak	8	501	44	12	31	55	105	4	1238
122	Moonstone Mountain Flank Steak with Brandy Sauce	3	733	53	13	47	58	187	1	638
123	Rattlesnake Creek Peppercorn Roast Beef*	10	414	46	5	23	50	128	<1	1772
124	Grilled Asian Prime Rib Rolls	3	346	28	25	13	33	71	3	1454
125	Mountain Home Marinated Steak*	4	629	28	16	51	72	68	<1	1112
126	Shoshone Sirloin in Red Wine Sauce	8	329	36	3	15	42	120	<1	141
127	Beef Stew with Red Wine and Polenta	6	763	62	47	32	39	189	5	1220
128	Curried Beef and Pasta in Tomato Sauce	6	667	29	69	32	43	97	8	1015
129	Oregon Trail Barbecued Lamb*	8	531	58	1	29	51	182	<1	411
130	Butterflied Idaho Spring Lamb with Lemon Mustard Sauce	10	482	62	1	24	46	213	<1	208
131	Thousand Springs Stir-Fried Lamb with Garlic	4	144	16	1	8	50	49	<1	223
132	Rack of Lamb in a Pecan Crust	4	1268	110	24	72	51	401	4	1336
133	Lamb Skewers with Balsamic Vinegar*	6	298	35	6	9	28	102	<1	567
134	Pork Chop Apple Bake	6	430	29	40	18	31	110	2	135
135	Braised Pork Loin with Red Onion, Cranberries and Cider	2	494	27	37	27	48	92	4	336
136	Hot Springs Marinated Pork*	8	534	49	11	35	57	134	<1	800
137	Pork Chops with Peppery Maple Bourbon Sauce*	4	625	32	25	39	56	170	<1	241
138	Crown Roast of Pork with Mushroom Stuffing	12	568	55	16	30	48	178	2	936
139	Pork and Red Peppers	4	414	40	7	21	45	108	1	444
140	City of Rocks Baby Back Ribs	2	457	28	26	26	52	104	1	2143

Page No.	Recipe Title	No. Servings	Cal	Prot (g)	Carbo (g)	T Fat (g)	% Cal From Fat	Chol (mg)	Fiber (g)	Sod (mg)
			Approximate Per Serving							
141	Garlic Pork Chops with Balsamic Vinegar	6	403	31	46	9	20	71	1	135
142	Pork Tnederloin à la Crème	4	713	33	11	55	69	241	1	2240
143	Pork Tenderloin with Bacon and Onion Sauce	4	669	53	18	41	55	195	2	947
144	Sausage and Wild Mushroom Lasagna	8	696	34	66	34	43	89	6	928
145	Red Pepper Sauce	8	182	8	15	11	52	21	4	260
145	Wild Mushroom Sauce	8	127	3	11	8	57	26	1	158
146	Veal Scallops with Sherry Sauce	3	535	31	19	33	55	126	1	556
147	Niagara Springs Elk Tenderloin with Caramelized Onions	8	549	52	3	31	51	222	1	477
148	Burgundy Elk en Croûte	12	281	18	22	12	39	81	2	401
149	Medallions of Venison with Gorgonzola Butter Sauce	4	988	43	3	89	81	239	<1	442
153	Rexburg Chicken Breasts with Balsamic Vinegar	2	448	24	11	35	69	129	<1	613
154	Braised Chicken with Mushrooms and Sun-Dried Tomatoes	4	374	39	18	13	30	91	4	461
155	Five-Spice Chicken with Cilantro*	4	169	29	5	3	17	73	<1	631
156	Lava Hot Springs Chicken and Garlic	4	489	52	13	23	42	158	2	813
157	Ginger Mustard Chicken	3	267	36	9	9	31	102	<1	624
158	Lookout Mountain Chicken	6	341	31	7	20	54	102	<1	457
159	Targhee Pass Chicken Scallops with Musartd Glaze	4	310	29	7	14	42	104	<1	468
160	Soda Springs Chicken and Stuffing	6	623	45	50	25	36	124	1	1633
161	Stuffed Chicken Breasts with Roasted Red Pepper Sauce	12	441	58	9	18	38	179	1	413
162	Idaho Falls Chicken Enchiladas	6	806	35	53	52	57	172	3	1582
163	Blackfoot Chicken and Barley Skillet Supper	6	284	20	30	9	29	50	6	497
164	Fort Hall Turkey Breast Scallopini	6	359	26	8	22	56	103	1	209
165	Marinated Cornish Hens*	4	1199	85	10	82	62	268	1	3054
166	American Falls Chukar with Mustard Sauce	4	1200	183	13	40	31	452	1	677
167	Henry's Fork Barbecued Duck*	2	1154	55	23	95	73	216	<1	8368
168	Marinated Duck with Port Sauce*	8	531	25	17	33	55	131	<1	567
169	Camas Duck Breasts with Walnut Salad	6	350	24	4	27	68	85	1	74
170	Pocatello Pheasant Au Vin	6	861	63	25	41	43	227	1	217

Page No.	Recipe Title	No. Servings	Cal	Prot (g)	Carbo (g)	T Fat (g)	% Cal From Fat	Chol (mg)	Fiber (g)	Sod (mg)
							Approximate Per Serving			
171	Fort Henry Cinnamon Pheasant	2	1176	102	43	58	44	331	2	2310
172	Breast of Pheasant with Fresh Sage	4	1042	97	51	46	41	323	2	326
173	Minnetonka Cave Pheasant Strips	4	657	91	10	25	35	226	1	373
177	Ernest Hemingway's Trout	6	426	45	9	22	48	138	<1	363
178	Moo Shu Salmon	4	670	33	70	28	38	218	6	1166
179	Trail Creek Balsdamic-Glazed Salmon	6	306	31	5	17	52	99	<1	164
180	Summer Salmon and Corn Relish with Basil Vinaigrette	4	713	45	38	45	55	119	9	243
181	River Run Herbed Sole Fillets	2	391	44	1	21	50	154	<1	409
182	Wood River Sole and Cabbage with Mustard Butter Sauce	2	644	28	22	50	69	117	3	629
183	Silver Creek Spring Trout with Wine and Herbs	4	555	63	2	29	49	188	<1	154
184	Sautéed Fish with Roasted Red Bell Pepper Sauce	2	520	51	29	21	36	91	3	4113
185	Linguini with Clam Sauce	4	691	36	71	26	35	125	2	977
186	Mussels with Plum Tomatoes	4	854	90	43	31	33	204	4	1071
187	Elkhorn Baked Scallops	6	412	16	29	26	56	94	1	1039
188	Pasta with Scallops and Tarragon	4	978	54	103	38	35	153	6	4014
189	Baker Creek Cabin Shrimp	6	317	29	15	17	46	211	3	1311
190	Baldy Shrimp and Scallop Sauté	6	273	24	10	15	50	140	2	343
191	Sun Valley Skiers Shrimp	4	201	19	13	7	31	158	2	895
192	Pasta with Shrimp, Tomatoes and Arugula	4	791	35	97	24	28	185	5	414
193	Seattle Ridge Seafood and Mushroom Casserole	8	459	23	17	34	65	194	2	1771
197	Whitewater Spicy Bean Cake	12	295	7	53	7	20	46	8	165
198	Chocolate Rum Cake with Rum Sauce	12	580	6	62	32	48	92	2	500
198	Sheepherder's Chocolate Cake	12	453	6	52	28	52	79	2	386
199	Redfish Lake Chocolate Devil with Raspberry Sauce	12	487	7	44	37	62	126	3	136
200	Challis Chocolate Zucchini Cake	12	402	5	51	21	46	60	2	179
201	Sawtooth Cranberry Gingerbread/Brown Sugar Whipped Cream	12	504	6	74	22	38	97	3	291
202	Flamed Orange Flan Cake	6	531	9	68	22	37	324	<1	240
203	Chocolate Chip Cookies with Walnuts and Raisins	96	98	1	11	6	55	15	<1	90

Page No.	Recipe Title	No. Servings	Cal	Prot (g)	Carbo (g)	T Fat (g)	% Cal From Fat	Chol (mg)	Fiber (g)	Sod (mg)
			Approximate Per Serving							
203	Float Trip Disappearing Chocolate Bars	9	271	3	43	11	35	24	2	119
204	Ranchers' Lemon Delights	24	53	<1	6	3	50	3	<1	26
205	White Chocolate Chip Cookies	48	165	3	20	9	49	31	1	96
206	Apple-Blueberry Crispy Cobbler	6	382	4	68	12	27	63	2	445
207	Almond Amaretto Cheesecake	16	388	8	25	28	63	115	3	211
208	Lemon Swirl Cheesecake	12	421	7	22	35	74	118	1	197
209	Individual Caramel Flans	12	261	7	46	6	21	152	0	171
210	Sherried Cream with Red Grapes	4	271	6	44	7	23	123	1	133
210	Crème Anglaise	2	947	12	61	74	69	663	<1	128
211	Lime Fool with Strawberries and Kiwifruit	4	530	5	52	36	58	91	4	64
212	Big Lost River Strawberries	6	414	3	51	24	50	62	3	113
212	Fresh Fruit with Sabayon Gratin	6	211	5	34	6	22	212	5	10
213	Steamed Persimmon Pudding	4	850	10	119	35	36	168	5	818
214	Salmon River Chocolate Pecan Pudding with Bourbon Sauce	8	466	9	33	33	62	276	2	201
215	Baked Rhubarb	6	310	2	42	16	45	42	2	240
215	Frozen Chocolate Pecan Pie	8	592	7	30	52	75	183	4	113
216	Eggnog Chiffon Pie	8	375	7	32	25	59	153	<1	188
217	Cream Cheese Banana Pie	8	430	8	51	23	46	49	1	274
217	Huckleberry Cream Cheese Pie	8	386	4	38	20	51	34	3	210
218	Pumpkin Sundae Pie	8	629	5	98	26	36	70	1	355
219	Puffed Apple Tarts	8	476	5	53	28	52	42	3	212
220	Custard Tart with Sautéed Pears	10	399	5	46	22	48	106	3	141
221	Raspberry Truffle Tart	10	523	4	61	31	51	76	5	49

* Nutritional profile includes marinade.

Wine Chart

Types of Wines		Cana	Carmela	Camas	Cocalalla	Indian Creek	Hells Canyon	Petros	Pintler	Rose Creek	South Hills	Ste. Chapelle	Vickers	Weston
Varietals White	Chardonnay	✓	✓	✓			✓	✓	✓✓	✓	✓	✓✓	✓	✓
	Chenin Blanc					✓			✓	✓	✓			
	Johannisberg Riesling	✓	✓	✓				✓	✓	✓	✓	✓		✓
	Late Harvest Riesling Dessert Wines						✓	✓		✓		✓		✓
	Gewürztraminer					✓					✓	✓		✓
	Semillion/Chardonnay						✓		✓					
	Sauvignon Blanc/Fume											✓		
	Muscat		✓											
	House			✓		✓								
Varietals Red	Merlot	✓	✓					✓				✓		
	Cabernet Franc		✓											✓
	Cabernet Sauvignon		✓	✓		✓	✓	✓	✓	✓		✓✓		✓
	Pinot Noir					✓		✓	✓	✓		✓		
	Lemberger		✓								✓			
	Syrah			✓								✓		
	House						✓							
Varietals Blush	White Pinot										✓			
	White Zinfandel													✓
	House		✓						✓	✓		✓		
Varietals Sparkling	Blanc de Blanc							✓						✓
	Brut											✓		
	Pinot Noir							✓				✓		
	Riesling											✓		
	Late Harvest											✓		
	House	✓			✓									✓

✓✓ Reserve + Varietal   There may be other specialty wines produced by each vintner.

Bibliography

Attebery, Louie B. *Idaho Folklife: Homesteads to Headstones.* University of Utah Press, Salt Lake City, Utah. Idaho Historical Society, Boise, Idaho.

Butruille, Susan G. *Women's Voices from the Oregon Trail.* Tamarack Books, Inc., Boise, Idaho, 1993.

Conley, Cort. *Idaho for the Curious.* Backeddy Books, Cambridge, Idaho, 1982.

Conley, Cort. *Idaho Loners, Hermits, Solitaries, and Individualists.* Backeddy Books, Cambridge, Idaho, 1994.

Conlin, Joseph R. *Bacon, Beans and Gallantines.* University of Nevada Press, Reno, Nevada, 1986.

Conlin, Joseph R. *Food and Foodways on the Western Frontier.* University of Nevada Press, 1986.

Harthorn, Sandy and Kathleen Bettis. *One Hundred Years of Idaho Art.* Boise Art Museum, 1990.

Hayes, Edith Goodwin. *Idaho Syringa.* American Guild Press, Dallas, Texas, 1956.

Heady, Eleanor B. *Sage Smoke: Tales of the Shoshoni-Bannock Indians.* Follett Publishing Company, Chicago, Illinois, 1973.

Idaho Nuggets. Compiled and published by the Idaho Writer's League, Inc., 1989.

Leitner, Della Adams. *White Gold.* Boise Printing Company, Boise, Idaho.

Martie, Elsie. *Salute to Pioneers of Washington and Adams Counties.* Council Publishing and Printing, Council, Idaho, 1984.

McFarland, Ronald E., ed. *Eight Idaho Poets: An Anthology.* The University Press of Idaho, Moscow, Idaho, 1979 (Page 65, Harald Wyndham, Poet).

Merrill, Irving R., ed. *Bound for Idaho.* The 1864 Trail Journal of Julius Merrill. The University of Idaho Press, Moscow, Idaho, 1988.

Nelson, Marjorie L. Ramey and Margaret DeMoss. *Footprints on Mountain Trails.* Arco Advertiser, Inc., Arco, Idaho, 1992.

Penson-Ward, Betty. *Idaho Women in History, Volume 1.* Legendary Publishing Company, Boise, Idaho.

Platt, Kenneth B. *Salmon River Saga.* Ye Galleon Press, Fairfield, Washington, 1978.

Scrimsher, Leda Scott. *Native Foods Used by the Nez Perce Indians of Idaho.* A thesis for the Degree of Master of Science, University of Idaho Graduate School, April 1967.

Sorrels, Rosalie. *Way Out in Idaho.* Confluence Press, Inc. Lewiston, Idaho, 1991.

Strahorn, Robert E. *Idaho Territory, 1881, The Resources and Attractions of.* Published by the direction of the Idaho Legislature, Special Act of the 11th Session, Boise City, Idaho, 1881.

Williams, Jacqueline. *Wagon Wheel Kitchens: Food on the Oregon Trail.* University Press of Kansas, Lawrence, Kansas, 1993.

Index of Contributors

Idaho à la cARTe Cookbook Committee and the Beaux Arts Société wishes to gratefully acknowledge the many individuals whose dedication, experience and commitment to quality have made this book possible.

Marti Agler
Anne Richey-Allen
Mickey Angell
Suzanne Attenborough
Betsy Ayers
Gail M. Baccheschi
Margie Baehr
Donna Bari
Arthur L. Barratt
Sue Barrett
Jan Bell
Jeanette Bennett
Helen Bohlin
Mary Bolen
Connie Bourman
Beth Brigham
Judy Burroughs
Linda Cadwell
Suzie Cagen
Harriet Calverley
Ann Carlson
Douglas Carnahan
Meredith Carnahan
Kelli Catron
Bethine Church
Carolyn Coffman
Genevieve Creswell
Lani Delvaque
Judy Dobson
Wanda Dowd
Barbara Emery
Barbara Erickson
Dorothy M. Ferron
Sydney Fidler

Joan Flint
Janice Forbes
Rebecca Fredericks
Marilyn Fredricks
Gretchen Hecht
    Friedman
Lynn Fritchman
Juliann Fritchman
Pat Fuji
Jude Garzolini
Wilna Gellert
Tonia Ginkel
Sybil Goade
Susan M. Graham
Diane Plastino Graves
Dorothy Hanford
Claude A. Hanson
Beverly Harad
Anne Hausrath
Tom Havey
Barbara Hawley
Alice Hayes
Hazel Haynes
Noreen Heist
Vicki Helming
Mary Henderson
Lola A. Herbots
Blanche Laure Herrick
Pauline Hinman
Pat Hoffman
Bonnie Hutchinson
Marilyn Hutchinson
Idaho Barley
    Commission

Idaho Bean
    Commission
Kay Jones
Linda Jones
Don Kayser
Mary Kayser
Shannon Keasler
JoAnn Keirn
Julie King
Karin King
Polly Read King
Jan Kinnas
Valene M. Klamt
C.F. Lancaster
Alice Lane
Becky Langhus
Heidi Layer
Lois M. Lenzi
Cynthia Lind
Judith C.
    Odmark-Britta
    Lindstrom
Jane Lloyd
Gerry Lumenello
Kass Manos
Laurel McClellan
Susan McConnell
Ginny McLafferty
Judy McRoberts
Joanne Merrill
Robert Meyer
Heidi Mickelson
Franky Mitchell
Penny Monger

Mary Morgan
Monica Morgan
Janet Morris
Gregory S. Naeve
Kaye Naeve
Pat Nelson
Judith Odmark
Dennis O'Leary
Jan Olivier
Susan Olson
Annette Park
Pat Patterson
Liven A. Peterson
Kathy Pidjeon
Lita Place
Patrick Pline
Julie Pool
Liz Questad
Jolene Quimby
Jen Ray
Charlene Ripke
Martha Ripple
Amy Rowe
Mildred E. Ruehlman
Suzy Ryder
Sylvia J. Sargeant
Betty Schultz
Marcia Selig
Bill Selvage
Shirley Severn
Bill Shaffer
Jane Shaffer
Gloria Shirley
Marilyn S. Slaby

Linda Payne Smith
Judith Smooke
Lucille Smylie
Lynn Snider
Nancy Sopwith
Joann Spence
Reneé Spengler
Jan Steele
Shirley Stenberg
Lois H. Stier
Melanie Stohner
Terry Stoltz
Mary Symms
Kathleen "Cookie"
    Terry
Carolyn Terteling
Elinor M. Thomas
Shirley W. Travis
Kathy Troutner
Terri Turpin
Naomi Tyler
Michelle Vinall
Mary Lou Wagner
Susan Waters
Barbara Watkins
Jenni Weltner
Gerda Weninger
Sharlyn Williams
Victoria Wodrich
Anne Work
Carol Writer

Index of Recipes

STEAKS
Bruneau Dunes Stuffed
    Flank Steak, 121
Moonstone Mountain Flank
    Steak with Brandy
    Sauce, 122
Mountain Home Marinated
    Steak, 125

STRAWBERRY
Big Lost River
    Strawberries, 212
Lime Fool with
    Strawberries and
    Kiwifruit, 211

STUFFINGS
Bruneau Dunes Stuffed
    Flank Steak, 121
Mushroom Stuffing, 138
Soda Springs Chicken and
    Stuffing, 160

TARTS
Custard Tart with Sautéed
    Pears, 220
Puffed Apple Tarts, 219
Raspberry Truffle Tart, 221

TOMATOES
Bogus Basin Broiled
    Tomatoes with
    Sherry, 97
Bruschetta Topping, 11
Cheese and Garlic-Stuffed
    Tomatoes, 24
Cream Cheese Spread with
    Sun-Dried Tomatoes
    and Basil, 31
Mussels with Plum
    Tomatoes, 186
Roasted Tomato Soup with
    Spinach Pesto, 72
Sacajawea Tomato and
    Green Bean Salad, 54

Tomatoes with Balsamic
    Vinegar and Provolone, 97

TOPPINGS
Brown Sugar Whipped
    Cream, 201
Bruschetta Topping, 11
Pecan Topping, 75

TORTILLAS
Cedar Street Tortilla
    Roll-Ups, 24
Gourmet Wrap-arounds, 26
Ponderosa Tortilla Soup, 71
Priest Lake Vegetable
    Wraps, 25

TROUT
Ernest Hemingway's
    Trout, 177
Kokanee Smoked Trout
    Mousse, 30

Silver Creek Spring Trout
    with Wine and
    Herbs, 183

TURKEY
Bonner's Ferry Smoked
    Turkey in Pumpkin
    Biscuits, 23
Cedar Street Tortilla
    Roll-Ups, 24
Fort Hall Turkey Breast
    Scallopini, 164
Turkey Wrap-arounds, 26

VEAL
Veal Scallops with Sherry
    Sauce, 146

VEGETABLES. *See also*
    Individual Kinds
Baked Vegetables
    Provençal, 89

Cataldo Mission Vegetarian
    Pizza Delight, 27
Priest Lake Vegetable
    Wraps, 25

VENISON
Medallions of Venison with
    Gorgonzola Butter
    Sauce, 149

WAFFLES
Turn-of-the-Century
    Waffles, 79

ZUCCHINI
Challis Chocolate Zucchini
    Cake, 200
Round Lake Zucchini and
    Rice Strudels, 28

M a i l   O r d e r   F o r m

Idaho à la cARTe
The Beaux Arts Société
670 South Julia Davis Drive
Boise, Idaho 83702
(208) 345-4542

	Price	Quantity	Total
	$24.95	_____	$ _____
	Shipping & handling $3.00 per book		$ _____
	Idaho residents add 5% sales tax		$ _____
	Total enclosed		$ _____

Name _____

Address _____

City/State/Zip _____

Telephone (   ) _____

Please charge my   [ ] Visa   [ ] MasterCard

Acct# _____

Expiration Date _____

Signature _____

Please make checks payable to Beaux Arts Société.
Please do not send cash.

Photocopies Accepted